Talkable Bible Stories

Larry Richards

Fleming H. Revell Company
Tarrytown, New York

Library of Congress Cataloging-in-Publication Data

Richards, Larry.
  Talkable Bible stories / Larry Richards.
     p. cm.
  Previously published as ch. 4 of: The Word parents handbook. c1983.
  Includes index.
  ISBN 0-8007-1660-4
  1. Bible stories, English.   I. Title.
[BS550.2.R52 1991]
220.9'505—dc20
                                              91-12923
                                                    CIP

Illustrations by Paul Richards.

Copyright © 1983, 1991 by Lawrence O. Richards
Published by the Fleming H. Revell Company
Tarrytown, New York 10591
Printed in the United States of America

Contents

Talkable Stories From the Gospels   141

Contents

What Are Talkable Bible Stories?

The Bible belongs to children as well as to adults. At times we hear, "The Bible is an adult book." In a way this is true. Many of the realities of our faith, expressed in great doctrines of the Scripture, are beyond the grasp of young children. But God's Word speaks powerfully to boys and girls as well as to adults. Truths they can understand—and experience—are imbedded in Bible stories which have been told and retold for thousands of years. The stories of the Bible are a vital part of our heritage. They speak in vivid, timeless images, revealing who God is, affirming his love for us, and teaching us how to respond to him and to one another.

The stories of the Bible capture vital truths and cast them in events which capture the imagination. Bible stories take root in our lives: Bible characters become our companions. The experiences of men and women, as reported in the two Testaments, help us to interpret our own lives and to understand God's work within us. It's no wonder, then, that as children begin to grow, we intuitively realize that the best way to teach them the Bible is to begin with Bible stories.

Reflecting on his own use of stories in treating children, the great child psychologist Bruno Bettelheim writes in *The Uses of Enchantment* (Random House, 1975) that "For a story to truly hold the child's attention, it must entertain him and arouse his curiosity. But to enrich his life, it must stimulate his imagination; help him to develop his intellect and to clarify his emotions; be attuned to his anxieties and aspirations; give full recognition to his difficulties, while at the same time suggesting solutions to the problems which perturb him. In short, it must at one and the same time relate to all aspects of his personality—and this without ever belittling but, on the contrary, while simultaneously promoting confidence in himself and his future" (p. 6). There is no greater resource for children than the stories of the Bible. Bible stories express the human condition and probe man's inner problems, yet explore them with a hope offered by their testimony to God, who speaks through them to young and old.

What Makes a Bible Event a "Story"?

Not every event reported in the Bible is a story. Every event does, of course, have significance—but not necessarily as a story. The sordid experience of Lot with his daughters after the destruction of Sodom has genealogical significance. It is a record of the origin of peoples who played a part in Israel's later history. But this event is not returned to again and again, to be told and retold by God's people as story. But other events reported in Scripture have been told and retold across the centuries. Why have some been focused on and not others? What makes certain events "stories"?

First, stories are those events which capture great truths about who God is and about our relationship with him. The Bible is God's unveiling of reality. It is his inspired picture of how we can live in this world in relationship with him and one another. We sense the timidity of Gideon, and watch as God encourages him until he becomes the leader of his people. We see Joseph face tragedy. Yet he remains faithful to God's standards and is finally exalted to be a ruler in Egypt. We see David, ashamed, confess his failure to God . . . and find healing in forgiveness. The great truths of Christian faith are explained in the sermons of the prophets and in the letters of the apostles. But these same truths are vividly illuminated, without sermon, in the stories of our Old and New Testaments. We do not build doctrine on Bible narrative. But through the stories of the Bible we teach powerfully the great revealed truths which hold meaning and hope for children as well as for adults.

Second, stories are events which bring us into relationship with Bible people. In the great stories of Scripture we meet people like ourselves. Their experiences help us to understand God's ways. Their faith sets us an example to follow. Their wrong choices stand as warnings. As we see God's role in the lives of believing men and women, we sense his presence in our own. Through the people of the Bible we discover how the great realities of our faith touch emotions, shape values, and guide behavior. The Bible friends that boys and girls make today will stay with them through their lives, continuing to give gentle guidance toward godliness.

Not every Bible story features human beings. Some, like the story of Creation, feature God's direct action. But most of the stories of the Bible feature men and women on whom children can model, whose lives touch them and teach them about God.

Third, Bible stories feature those events which teach us about ourselves. The most powerful Bible stories illuminate our own lives. We can explore our feelings as we sense the emotions of Daniel, pressured to conform to pagan ways in the king of Babylon's school. We can grow more sensitive to others as we see the compassion of Jesus. Through Bible stories the basic values which infuse our lives can be examined, chosen, and become part of our character. Bible stories can be one of the most effective means that God uses to guide children's personal growth.

All this helps explain the principle of selection which underlies the choice of Old and New Testament stories for this book. The stories that have been chosen are each related to childhood anxieties and aspirations. Each story is linked with specific childhood "problems" which are, in fact, unique opportunities for moms and dads to provide distinctive Christian nurture.

The stories in this book are familiar ones. But each is retold in special ways to highlight its linkage with the experiences of your boys and girls. These specially selected, specially retold Bible stories were chosen because of the unique way each may touch the life of your own six- to eleven-year-old.

How to Tell Bible Stories

We've all seen the gifted storyteller who can hold a crowd of children in rapt fascination. But storytelling at home is not for the crowd. It's for intimate moments spent with a single child, or for warm times when your family is gathered around. At times like these, stories are not for just telling. They are for sharing. In family adventures with Bible stories, children are participants and not just listeners.

That's why this book suggests different ways to share Bible stories with your boys and girls. There are ideas here to help you act out stories, living them together in that "pretend" way which is so real to the young. There are ideas for one activity associated with each story; an activity to help you carry the story truths over into daily life. And, with each story, there are talkable suggestions; suggestions for you to pause and chat with your children about what's happening in the story and how it relates to their own experiences.

In a sense the art of family storytelling means joining hands with your children, going together to visit people of the Bible, and then bringing the truths you learn together back to enrich your experience as a family.

This is just the way stories were used in Bible times. We see the principles of family Bible teaching in a famous Old Testament passage. After calling God's people to love and honor the Lord, the writer gives a simple prescription for teaching children. The instructions are directed to parents, and they begin with the adult response to the Lord. God's words to us, the Bible says, ". . . are to be upon your hearts. Impress them on your children. . . . Talk about them when you sit at home and when you walk along the road, when you lie down and when you get up" (Deuteronomy 6:6, 7). We can see three principles in these instructions.

(1) We are to take God's Word into our own hearts. We are to open our lives to the Lord, to let the teachings and the stories of the Bible shape our personalities. As we are being shaped, we have the privilege of sharing what we experience with our families.

(2) God's Word is to be taught in families. The ideal context for responding to the Bible is found in the close, warm, constant relationships provided by the home. As children learn about God from those they love and trust, and sense parents' love for the Lord, they readily respond to him.

(3) God's Word is to be woven into the fabric of our lives together. Bible teaching isn't just for special, set-aside times in which we mimic the school. Instead, Bible stories are to be linked with daily life—related to the experiences of our boys and girls. It's easy to see why this kind of teaching can be so powerful. When we sense fear in a child, we have an opportunity to hold him close—and to share a Bible story which builds trust in God. When we're disturbed by outbursts of anger, we can turn together to Bible stories which help a child explore his own feelings and learn godly responses. When we observe a fault, another story from the Bible helps explore similar flaws in Bible people, and find better ways to live. Only in the family can the use of Bible stories be so intimately woven into daily life, for the needs of a child are best sensed by loving parents.

So family storytelling is unique. It features intimate moments of sharing together the great, life-shaping stories of the Bible. And our closeness to our children helps us select just those Bible stories which our boys and girls most need to help them grow.

How Children Understand the Bible

Many studies by child psychologists have shown something most of us realize. Children do not think or understand as adults do. Just as a five-year-old's body does not permit him to play ball with the skill of a teen, so his "mental muscles" have not developed to the place where he is able to think as a youth or adult.

Generally, the thinking of children between the ages of four and seven can be characterized as "intuitive." Words are still personal, and represent what the child has experienced and perceived. A child in this stage of mental development makes little distinction between times and places. There is no sense of gap, for instance, between the time of Abraham and of Christ. To young boys and girls, everything seems "now" and "here."

Children between seven and ten are generally found in the stage of "concrete" thinking. Now children can begin to take the point of view of others, and compare others' feelings and perspectives with their own. Now, too, boys and girls can look ahead, and see the consequences of actions. They can decide ahead of time what they will do, and can understand what their choices will mean.

Older children, generally between the ages of ten and fifteen, reach the stage of "formal operational" thinking. Now they can analyze: now they are able to explore relationships between the real and the possible. Now many "adult" kinds of thinking become possible.

Some educators have examined the ways that children think and have concluded that, because of a young boy's and girl's mental limitations, we should not teach them the Bible. These people argue that to "really understand" the Bible calls for kinds of thinking of which boys and girls are not yet capable. They fear that if we teach them the Bible too young, children will actually misunderstand, and build impressions they need to unlearn later.

But these fears are based on a radical misunderstanding of the nature of God's Word. Certainly the Bible presents concepts and ideas children cannot grasp intellectually. But the Bible does more than present concepts. The Bible unveils realities which God's people are invited to experience! A five-year-old may not understand forgiveness. But he can certainly grasp the fact that God loves and forgives him, and experience the release that forgiveness brings. A nine-year-old may not grasp the mystery of incarnation in an adult way. But she can know that God's Son came into our world, lived here, and that because he became like us he fully understands both her joys and her sorrows.

So our goal in teaching the Bible to children is not to help them master Bible doctrine in an adult, schooled way. Our goal in teaching the Bible to children is to help boys and girls grasp the practical meaning of those Bible truths which they can experience in their daily life now.

In teaching Bible stories we are not trying to link doctrines to abstract ideas. We are trying to link the great truths of our faith with the sights and sounds of daily life. Our goal is to communicate Bible truths as realities which will become the framework of our child's world.

How important such Bible stories are. Stories are not abstract statements. Stories are flesh-and-blood expressions of God's truths. Your children may not understand doctrines in an adult way. But as you share Bible stories with them, in ways fitted to their stage of growth and matched to their personal experiences, your boys and girls will come to know God. They will come to know about him in ways that are deeply meaningful to them.

The stories retold in this book are shaped in words and phrases which fit the thinking of the ages for which they are intended. *Talkables* and *action ideas* further link the stories to daily life. Told and retold in your home, these Bible stories *will* help your children grasp great Bible truths. And these stories will help them come to love and respond to God.

How to Use These Bible Stories

Each Bible story is keyed to specific childhood experiences and needs. And each story is organized in a simple, three-part way.

Background. The background capsulizes the story and its key truths, and identifies the times when it is especially appropriate for you to tell the particular story. In addition, the background indicates numbered paragraphs in the first three chapters which discuss those childhood needs to which the story is related.

The Story Retold. Each Bible story is retold in words appropriate to the age-group and the way children think. You can read the story to the children from this book. Or you can read the story ahead of time, and tell it in your own way. However, remember that the story is retold to highlight the needs which it meets.

One of the most important features of the retelling is built into each story. This feature is the *talkable.* Sometimes *talkables* focus on values, to help you share what is important to you in a life-shaping way. Sometimes *talkables* focus on the feelings of Bible men and women, and on similar feelings experienced by you and your children. Sometimes a talkable explores behavior, to help your children think about choices they will make. Always talkables encourage you and your children to share with each other and with the Lord.

There's one thing that is very important to understand about talkables. Their suggestions are to help your children share. *But they are also to help you share with your children!* You'll often find that you need to take the lead in responding first to a talkable suggestion.

Your personal sharing is a vital part of family Bible teaching. You see, we adults are models for our children. Much of what our boys and girls learn does not come from our preaching but from our example. Thus we want to share our faith with our children, and talk freely about our attitudes and values and our own experiences, so they can learn from us. When we communicate our values and beliefs and our feelings as we, too, respond to the Bible stories, we transmit a living faith to our next generation.

Action Idea. This is another unique feature. With most stories a simple follow-up activity idea is included. These ideas are optional. You don't have to use them when you tell the story. But you can use them if you want.

What Responses Can I Expect?

Growing up is a process. No childhood needs are met in a moment, nor are the problems of boys and girls solved instantly. While we yearn to see progress in the lives of our children, we must remember that growth is a slow process. This is certainly true in the physical realm. We may not even notice how much our child has grown until we compare a picture taken six months or a year ago, and suddenly realize how much he's changed! So we shouldn't be surprised if growth in the psychological, social, and spiritual realms is also a gradual kind of thing.

When you notice something in one of your children that troubles you, look it up in the index of this book. You'll find two things. First, there will be discussion of the problem area, and how it can become an opportunity for Christian nurture. Second, one or more Bible stories which have special value in helping a child gain insight and find God's guidance will be identified. You'll find ideas of what to do in the coming weeks or even months to provide supportive guidance.

Sometimes retelling a Bible story may stimulate no response from our child at all. For some reason he or she simply does not seem ready, or sense its relevance. In this case it's best to wait a couple of weeks, or wait for a particular happening, then sit down immediately and retell the story. This time the incident may create the readiness.

Sometimes children will be able to respond and apply the story insights immediately. At other times the truths shared may germinate for further weeks, and you may talk of the story several more times before you see responsiveness and change. *It is particularly important to be very patient during such germination times.* You and I are not to use the Bible to club a child, or to impose demands that he or she conform. We are to use Bible stories as gentle words from God: loving words spoken by the Holy Spirit, lovingly providing insight and hope. We too must be patient and loving and gentle, and share helpful Bible stories as a doorway to hope rather than a nagging demand for change.

One indication that a Bible story is having an impact in a child's life is his request to return to it. "Tell me again about Moses dying," a child who has lost a grandparent may ask in the weeks following the death. Returning to the story is one of the clearest of indications that God's Spirit is quietly working through the Word, helping the child deal with a disturbing event in his life.

At other times you *will* see changes, soon. The child who was afraid of the dark hears an appropriate Bible story, draws a picture of it for his wall, and in a week or so begins to go to bed without the anxiety which had gripped him before. How enriching that is, to see such quick and clear evidence of the touch of God's hand.

What is important for you and me to remember, whether the response we see is quick or delayed, is that what we are sharing with our boys and girls is the very, living Word of God. God is someone you and I can trust implicitly. We can trust his timing. We can trust his Spirit to work through his reliable Word, to help us nurture the growing personalities of the children that we—and God—so dearly love.

TALKABLE STORIES FROM GENESIS

God Creates
Genesis 1

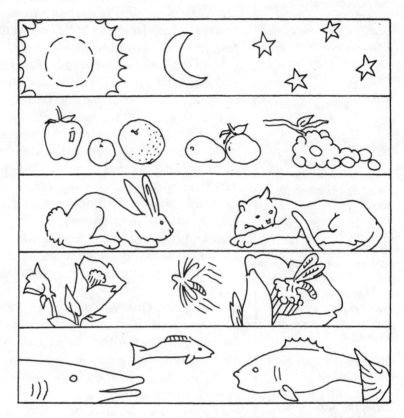

What is the best thing God made?

Background The Genesis message is that we live in a personal universe. Our world was not shaped by mindless forces. It was lovingly designed by a personal God, to be home for humanity. The pattern and order of creation stand as witnesses: the very regularity of day following day, of season following season, show that the world was planned to provide a stable framework for human life, and give us a sense of security.

How important for our children to sense the essential friendliness of God's universe. Despite sin's impact on nature, God's loving hand can still be seen. Every boy and girl can hear in this mighty Genesis passage the wonderful message that he or she is important, the object of God's special care. This story is retold especially for your younger boys and girls.

[1] *What are some of the good things about day? What are some of the things we like about night? How hard it would be for us to sleep if the sun was bright all the time. God made the night to help us rest.*

[2] *How many different ways do we enjoy the plants and foods God made? (For instance, beauty, shade from trees, good taste, satisfying hunger, vitamins, etc.) What is your favorite fruit or vegetable? Do you think God knew that you would enjoy the (fill in favorite food) when He planned it?*

[3] *What do you think night would be like without the moon or the stars? How would you feel at night without them? When we look out the window at night and see the moon or the stars, we know that God is there. What words tell how you feel when you see them, and know that God is near?*

[4] *What's your favorite of the birds God made? Why does this bird seem special to you?*

Long ago, before God made the world, He thought and thought. God wanted the world to be special, because He had an exciting plan. Do you know what that plan was? God planned to make people, like you and me, whom He could love. God wanted the world His people would live in to be just right.

Finally, when God was ready, He created the heavens and the earth. He began to shape them into a special home for us. Here's what the Bible tells us God did.

The very first thing, God spoke and said, "Let there be light!" And everywhere there was a warm, bright glow, shining in the air. But God knew that you and I would need darkness too. So God planned for times when the light would go away, and there would be night. God saw what He had done in making day and night, and He smiled. It was good.[1]

At first the world was covered with thick, wet clouds. Then God spoke again. Most of the water settled down to cover the ground, and the deep blue sky appeared.

Then God gathered the water together into oceans and lakes and streams. And the dry land appeared. With another word, God covered the land with grass and flowers and trees. All the vegetables we like to eat, and all the fruits that grow on trees, were made for us by God. God looked around at what He had made and smiled. It was good.[2]

When God spoke again it was to set lights in the sky. The two great lights that God made are the sun, for daytime, and the moon, for nighttime. God made the stars, too, and placed everything just right so we would have our seasons: our spring and summer, and fall and winter. God planned it all. We can count on God's sun coming up every morning. When winter is cold, we know spring and summer will come again.[3]

God made a beautiful world for men and women and boys and girls. But the world still seemed empty. So God spoke again. This time He filled the waters with fish, and created birds to fly in the sky and nest in the trees.[4]

Then God spoke one more time. He filled the world with all kinds of animals. He looked carefully at all He had done, and God smiled, because it was good.

But God had one more thing to do. God had planned the world as a place for people to live. God had filled the world with beautiful things. He had made fish and birds and animals for us to enjoy. Now God made the most special thing of all. Gently and lovingly, God shaped the first man and woman!

God made them very special. He made them in His own image and likeness. Only human beings are like God. Like God, we can think and understand. Like God, we can feel, and love others. Like God, we can know what's right and wrong, and can choose to do what is right.

No animals are this special. Only people are made in God's image, to be like Him in these special ways.

When God had finished creating, He gave everything in the world to us to take care of for Him. God was very happy with what He had done, for it was very good.[5]

[5]How does it make you feel to know that you are special to God? What are special things about each member of our family that you think must please God? God loves each of us very much. Each of us is very special to God.

> ***Action Idea*** To strengthen the sense of specialness, try keeping a "special" diary for a week. Jot down unique things each child says or does. Afterward, read each the list of special things about him that you jotted down. Let each child know how pleased you are with him or her, and pray together. Thank God that your children are even more special to God than they are to you.

God Makes Us Special
Genesis 2

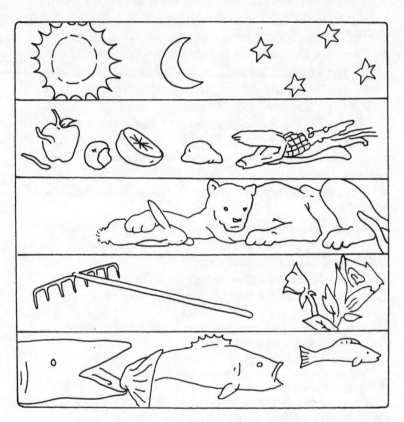

What special things can people do?

Background   Genesis 2 describes Eden, the garden God shaped for the first pair. The account is fascinating, for it shows how carefully God designed Eden to exercise every capacity of personhood. God Himself enjoyed beauty, engaged in meaningful work, expressed creativity, sought fellowship, and exercised moral choice. Genesis 2 shows us that God carefully planned Eden to enable human beings, made in His image and likeness, to exercise these same capacities.

When God created Adam, God made him very special. The Bible says God created man in His own image. God made people to be like Him in very special ways.

For instance, God can think and understand. So can you and I. God can feel happy, or sad. So can you and I. God can love others, just as we can love.

When God created Adam, God wanted Adam to have the joy of using all the wonderful and special abilities Adam had been given. So God planned a special garden for Adam to live in. He called the garden Eden. God let Adam live in the garden, to discover just how special Adam was.[1]

When God made the garden, He planted all kinds of trees in it. God chose trees that would look beautiful, because God enjoys beautiful things. And God chose trees for the garden that had delicious fruit on them: fruit God knew would taste good to Adam. So when Adam walked through the garden, he was thrilled with the beauty. And he enjoyed the taste of many different kinds of fruit.[2]

When God put Adam in the garden, He did a very wonderful thing. He told Adam that from now on Adam could take care of the garden. God had worked when He created the world, and knew how good it felt to do a job well. Do you remember? The Bible says God looked around at the things He had done, and saw that it was good. Well, God wanted Adam to have that same joy. So he let Adam work in the garden and take care of it. Maybe Adam decided to plant flowers in new patterns. Or Adam planned to put a hedge beside one of the rivers. Now Adam could do what he wished to make the garden look just the way he wanted. Then Adam could feel good about the work he had done.[3]

God had made all the animals and birds, but God did not name them. He left that for Adam to do. God knew how good it felt to create—to make something fresh and new and special. So He wanted Adam to have the fun of making up something fresh and new and special

[1]What do you suppose you would have seen or done in the Garden of Eden? What are some of the things you would have learned about yourself? Which things you did would have made you happiest? Why?

[2]You're special like Adam, because you can enjoy beautiful things. Let me tell you about the most beautiful thing I ever saw. Then you tell me about the most beautiful thing you ever saw.

What are some kinds of fruit that you've eaten? Which do you like best? Would you like to come to the store with me sometime and see if we can find fruit you've never tasted?

[3]What work do you do that you're proud of? Do you think doing your school work is like the work Adam had to do, or not like it? Why? (Share what makes work that you do satisfying.)

[4]Can you think of
anything special you
have made up yourself?
(Remind your child of a
poem written, or a
picture drawn, or an
imaginative story told,
etc.)

too. God let Adam make up the names. Making up the
names was making up something very new and special.[4]

But something was still missing. You see, God made
Adam so he would need another person to love. God
wanted Adam to learn that having others to love is very
important. Finally, when Adam knew that something
was missing, God had Adam fall asleep. God took one of
Adam's ribs and, just as God had shaped Adam, God
made a woman, named Eve.

When God brought Eve to Adam, Adam knew immediately what she was. "Here is a person just like me!"
Adam said, and called her "woman." Now Adam would
have another person who could also love beauty and be
proud of work and make up fresh, new things, to share
with. Adam would never be alone again.

Later, when Adam and Eve had children, there were
other persons to share the wonderful world God had
made. And all the children, like Adam and Eve, could
enjoy beauty, and feel proud of their work, and make up
things fresh and new.

You see, you are special too. God gave us many special abilities, and there are many wonderful things you
and I can do.

Action Idea Be alert for chances to praise your child
for work done well. Also express appreciation for any
creative efforts. You can also stimulate a number of
shared projects. Use this story to launch a younger
child on family chores. Let him or her choose from
several possibilities, asking which would give the greatest satisfaction.

Adam and Eve Are Tempted
Genesis 3

Are you happier when you do right or when you do wrong?

Background The temptation theme occurs often in Scripture. While we are not to seek out such tests, it is wrong to view temptations as evils. In fact, those moments of conflict between our desire to do what is right, and the pull toward a different choice, are moments which can actually strengthen our commitment to God. Every choice of God's way builds our moral character.

Genesis describes God placing the Tree of Knowledge of Good and Evil in the Garden of Eden. The tree planted in Eden, and God's command not to eat its fruit, was actually a great gift. Because the tree was there, and Adam and Eve had a choice, they could live as responsible moral agents. Without the presence of that tree, and thus opportunity to choose, the first pair would have been puppets of flesh, not true human beings.

In this Bible story about the weeks, months, and perhaps years before the sin reported in Genesis 3, you can help your children explore some of the great truths which protect us when we are tempted and encourage us to choose God's way.

23

Life was good for Adam and Eve in the Garden called Eden. God had made the garden, and He planned it to be very special. God planted the garden with beautiful trees, filled with tasty fruit. God let Adam and Eve take care of the garden. They probably planted special plots of flowers, and arranged the bushes just the way they wanted them. Adam and Eve had friendly birds and animals for company. And they had each other to love.

There was one other very special thing about the garden. It was the most special thing of all. Evenings, God often came to be with Adam and Eve in the garden.

There was one other thing about the garden. God planted one special tree in the garden. And God gave Adam and Eve one command. "Don't eat any of the fruit from that one tree," God said.

God even explained. God told them that if they disobeyed Him, and ate, the fruit of that tree would make them die. Adam and Eve didn't understand what "die" meant. But they knew that something very bad would happen if they disobeyed God.

We don't know how long Adam and Eve lived happily in the beautiful Garden of Eden. We don't know how many times they walked together, hand in hand, past the tree God warned them about. They must have looked at it many times. But they never touched it. Adam and Eve knew God loved them. They knew that doing what God told them not to do would hurt them. The tree looked beautiful. Its fruit looked tasty. The fruit even smelled very good. Adam and Eve may even have wanted to taste it. But they didn't. They turned away from it. And when they did, Adam and Eve must have felt very, very good.[1]

How do you feel when you know you've done the right thing instead of something wrong or bad? How do you think Adam and Eve felt when they turned away from the tree?

When are you most likely to be tempted to do something you know isn't right? (Share a temptation from your own childhood.) What helps you to do the right thing when you feel tempted?

Why do you suppose Adam and Eve wanted to do the right thing, and to please God? Let me tell the story again. You listen for things that would help Adam and Eve to obey God. (Focus on evidence that God loved them, and wanted only the best for them.)

Action Idea   If your child has told about a personal temptation, there's a simple thing you can do to help him or her resist.

For children from six to eleven you might cut out a construction paper tree, and a number of round, red "fruit." The tree can be taped to the wall of the child's room, or to a family bulletin board, or to the refriger-

24

ator door. Whenever your child resists the temptation he has told about, he can tape a fruit to the tree. Giving in to the temptation means a fruit should be taken off. At the end of a week, or after several days, talk about each fruit on the tree and your child's victories. Express your own pleasure and pride.

Adam and Eve Sin
Genesis 3

Can you find Adam and Eve? When do people want to hide from others?

Background The story of the Fall tells how sin entered our world and tainted the human race. Subsequent history demonstrates the tragic outcome . . . in injustice, war, and in the personal experience of every individual.

While the Genesis report traces the origin of our subjection to sin back to Adam and Eve, it never suggests that individuals today are not responsible for their actions. We each make choices, which mirror the choice of Eve and Adam. Like them, we too experience natural consequences of wrong doing, as suggested in this Genesis chapter.

A dam and Eve lived together in a beautiful place, planned just for them by God.

In the whole, big, beautiful garden where they lived there was only one thing Adam and Eve could not do. God had planted one tree in the garden whose fruit they were not to eat. God warned Adam and Eve. "If you eat that fruit, you will begin to die." Adam and Eve didn't know just what that meant. But they did know that something terrible would happen if they ate the fruit God warned them against.[1]

For a long time Adam and Eve obeyed God. They didn't touch the fruit of that tree. But one day, when Eve was alone, Satan came in disguise and talked with her. Satan, who was God's enemy, tried to make Eve doubt God.

"Did God really say you're not to eat that fruit?" he asked. And then Satan lied to Eve. Satan tried to make her think God didn't love her and Adam. Satan said, "Terrible things won't really happen if you eat the fruit. God doesn't want you to have the fruit because it will be good for you."

Eve looked at the fruit and smelled it. It was beautiful, ripe fruit. It looked as if it would taste delicious. And Eve wanted to find out for herself what would happen if she ate it.

So she did!

Then she gave some to Adam. And Adam ate the fruit too.[2]

As soon as Adam and Eve ate the fruit, they knew they'd done wrong. They looked at each other and they felt ashamed.

Later, when God came to the garden to walk with them, Adam and Eve ran away and hid. They felt guilty and afraid.[3]

When God found Adam and Eve they were trying to hide. God was very sad. "Have you eaten from the tree I told you not to eat from?" God asked. God knew the answer. But He wanted to give Adam a chance to admit what he had done. Instead Adam blamed Eve. "She gave

[1] *Why do you suppose God warned them not to eat the fruit of that tree? Do you think eating it would be a good thing for them or a bad thing? What are some of the things you're not supposed to do because they would be bad for you?*

[2] *How do you think Adam and Eve felt after they ate the fruit? How do you feel when you do something you know is wrong?*

[3] *Something happens inside us when we do wrong. We begin to feel bad about ourselves. Can you think of a time when you felt ashamed and guilty and afraid?*

[4] Do you think those were good excuses? Whose fault is it if we do something we know is wrong?

me the fruit," Adam said. And Eve blamed Satan. "He tricked me," Eve said.[4]

God was sad. He told Adam and Eve what would happen now because they had disobeyed. Adam and Eve would have to leave the Garden of Eden. They would have to work hard, because weeds would come up now as well as vegetables and fruit. And that very day Adam and Eve began to grow old. One day they would die.

Adam and Eve hadn't known all the things that would happen if they disobeyed God. But God knew. God had told them what to do because He loved them. How much better it would have been for Adam and Eve if they had chosen to do right instead of wrong.

Action Idea Wise parents establish few rules, and those that are established are for the child's benefit. Coming home after school before going to another's house to play, doing homework before going to another's house to play, doing homework before bedtime, and picking up one's own clothes—these are simple regulations without great moral content. But they do have significant value to the child.

God Calls Abraham
Genesis 12:1–9

Does Sarah look happy to move?

Background Abraham was a prosperous pagan merchant in the magnificent ancient city of Ur. Joshua identifies Abraham's time as a day when the forefathers "lived beyond the River and worshiped other gods" (24:2). Yet when God the Creator spoke to Abraham, the 75-year-old merchant responded to the Lord's voice.

Today about one family in five in the United States moves each year. It's always hard for children to leave friends and familiar places for the unknown. Sharing the story of Abraham and discussing his move can stimulate your children to share their worries and concerns. And you can remind your children that God will be with your family wherever you go.

This Bible story is told in the form of a skit. You can read each part, or let older children in the family put it on for the rest of the family.

29

(Door slams, run in place.)

Abram: (breathlessly) Sarah! Sarah! Lot!

Sarah: My goodness, Abram. What's the matter?

Abram: Whew! ... Just a minute. Let me catch my breath.

Sarah: Here, sit down. Why, running like that at your age. You'll have a heart attack!

Abram: But Sarah, it's so exciting. Where's Lot?

Lot: I'm here, Uncle Abram.

Abram: Listen, both of you. We're going to move!

(Sarah and Lot together:)

Sarah: Move! *Lot:* What, leave Ur?

Abram: That's right. Sarah, it's the most exciting thing. God just spoke with me!

Sarah: What, Nannar our moon god ...?

Abram: No. No, not Nannar. The true God. The God who made the whole world, and human beings too.

Lot: But we don't know any God like that.

Abram: Well, I know Him now. The true God spoke to me, and told me to move. So we're moving.

Sarah: Where are we going?

Abram: I don't know. But God will tell me when we get there.

Lot: But ...

Abram: And listen. God gave me wonderful promises. He promised to bless me, and make our family a great nation. God is going to protect us, and somehow all the peoples of the world will be blessed because I know God, and obey Him.

Sarah: (doubtfully) Well, if you're sure ...

Abram: I'm sure. God spoke to me, and told me to move. And God is going to be with us, family. O there are such good things ahead for us!

Sarah: Well, I guess we'd better get ready to go.

Lot: Uncle Abram, what should we pack?

Abram: Bring everything. Our herds. Our money. All your dresses, Sarah. All our servants. And Lot ...

Lot: Yes, Uncle Abram.

Abram: Lot, buy lots of tents.

Sarah: Tents!

Abram: That's right. We'll live in tents from now on. We can't bring our brick air-conditioned houses, you know.

Sarah: (unhappy) But I don't want to live in a tent.

Abram: Don't worry, Sarah. God is sending us. And God will be with us. O Sarah, I just know there are such good things ahead![1]

Thank God He cares for us today, just as He cared for Abraham.

Action Idea Pretend with your children that God has spoken to you as He did to Abraham. You are going to move . . . in just one hour!

Have each family member take a paper grocery sack. Each of you has just five minutes to select things to bring along, and put them in the sack. Take what is important to you, but only what will fit in the sack. Everything else must be left behind. When time is up, show each other what you packed. Tell why each item is important to you. Then tell about anything that was especially hard to think of leaving behind.

[1]*How did each person feel about moving? Why do you think each felt the way he or she did?*

What's the hardest thing for you about moving?

Why do you think it was easier for Abram to plan to move than for Sarah and Lot?

Can you think of some hard things it's easier for us to do because we trust God, as Abram did? (Recall and share individual as well as family experiences.)

Abraham Fails to Trust God
Genesis 12:10–20, 20:1–18

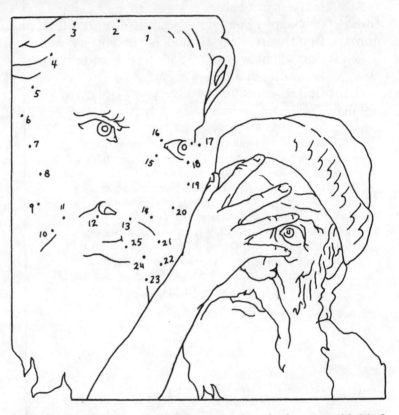

Would Abraham be afraid if he remembered who was with him?

Background Abraham was a man of faith. But at times he too was fearful and failed to trust God. The Book of Genesis reports two incidents of fear that rulers would kill Abraham in order to marry his wife, Sarah.

Children also are often gripped by fears of what might happen. They imagine monsters in their closets, ghosts outside their window, lions and tigers prowling the neighborhood.

Some boys and girls just starting school are afraid of what they will find there. Older boys and girls may beat them up. The teacher may not like them. They may find no friends. All these are natural anxieties. Such fears are very real to our boys and girls. Like Abraham, our children may need to be reminded many times that when we know God, we do not have to be terrified of things that "might" lie ahead.

32

Abraham had left his home in Ur when God told him to move. It must have been a hard thing for Abraham to do, leaving everything he knew to go to a place he had never been.[1]

Yes, Abraham probably was worried. But Abraham trusted God enough to obey Him. Finally Abraham did come to the land we call Israel. There were some cities in the land. But there were great empty fields and high, grassy hills too. Abraham traveled slowly across the new land and saw how beautiful it was. His flocks of sheep and herds of cattle grew. Abraham became even richer than he had been in Ur, his old home. God took good care of Abraham and everything Abraham owned.

But when Abraham pitched his tents in the southern part of Israel near a town called Gerar, Abraham began to worry. You see, Abraham's wife, Sarah, was very beautiful. Everyone thought she was the most beautiful woman they had ever seen. So Abraham began to imagine all sorts of terrible things that might happen. *Maybe,* Abraham thought, *the king of Gerar will want to marry Sarah!* And Abraham imagined what might happen then. Why, what if the king decided to kill Abraham so he could marry Sarah! What if the king's soldiers attacked him? The more Abraham thought about the terrible things that might happen, the more he was afraid.[2]

What Abraham did then was foolish. He didn't stop to think that God would take care of him. Instead, Abraham told a lie, and made Sarah promise to lie too.

"This is my sister," Abraham said when he introduced Sarah. He was afraid to tell people Sarah was really his wife.

Well, the king of Gerar was very excited. He *did* want to marry Sarah, and had her come to his palace. Now Abraham and Sarah were really in trouble![3]

Abraham and Sarah were in deep trouble. Sarah was at the king's palace. And Abraham was even more afraid than ever. How could he go and tell the king he had lied?

Abraham had forgotten to trust God. But God still

[1]*Do you think Abraham might have been worried or afraid when he started out? What are some of the things Abraham might have been afraid of?*

[2]*What else do you suppose Abraham might have imagined that would frighten him? Do you think Abraham was wise to be so scared of something that might happen, but might never happen at all?*

[3]*Have you ever been so afraid of something you told a lie instead of the truth? What happened then? (Share an experience of your own when you were afraid and acted unwisely.)*

took care of Abraham. God spoke to the king of Gerar in a dream, and warned the king that Sarah was already married. God kept the king from actually marrying Sarah. And God told the king to send Sarah back to Abraham right away.

Sometimes you and I forget God is with us, and imagine all sorts of things to be afraid of. But even when we forget God, He doesn't forget us. God is always with us, just as He was with Abraham even when Abraham was afraid.

> *Action Idea*   Often children find it easier to talk about their own fears as if they were fears of someone else. Work together to make a list of things that the classmates of your child or children might be afraid of. Post the list on a family bulletin board. Include God's promise to Abraham, recorded in Genesis 15:1. "Do not be afraid, Abram. I am your shield."

Abraham and Lot
Genesis 13

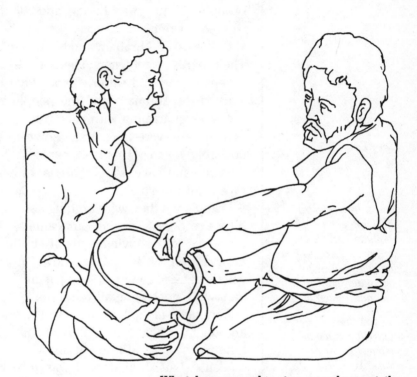

What happens when two people want the same thing?

Background   Abraham and Lot were family: uncle and nephew. Yet tensions developed between them over their possessions. In a passage which begins and ends with a description of Abraham at worship (13:3, 4 and 13:18), we discover the godly way that Abraham dealt with a problem which is common in modern families.

While some quarreling is natural and even healthy between children, children also need to explore their feelings and find better ways than angry bickering to resolve their disputes.

Undoubtedly Abraham's confidence in God's love for him was a freeing influence. When our children are reassured of our love, and of God's care, it is easier for them to surrender their "rights" for the sake of brothers and sisters, and of peace.

When God told Abraham to move, he left his home in Ur. Abraham gathered everything he owned—his herds, and his cattle, and the people who worked for him—and Abraham set out for a new country. Abraham's nephew, Lot, came along with him. Lot also brought all his own herds, and all the people who worked for him.

God blessed Abraham and his family in the new land. Their herds got bigger. There were more and more sheep to feed and water. Before long the people who worked for Abraham and the people who worked for Lot were quarreling with each other!

"Hey! We were here first," some of Lot's herdsmen probably yelled. "This is our grass!"

"You can't have it all," Abraham's herdsmen argued. "We want our share."

Pretty soon they were arguing about water too. "Wait till we're done watering our camels," Lot's herdsmen may have said, shoving some of Abraham's sheep away from a well. "It's our turn now!" Abraham's herders yelled back. "You're hogging it all!" Before long the men were quarreling all the time![1]

Abraham was unhappy about the quarreling. A little arguing might have been all right. But quarreling all the time wasn't a good thing at all![2]

Well, what Abraham did was this. He came to his nephew Lot and said, "Let's not have any quarreling between you and me, or between your herdsmen and mine, for we're family." And Abraham had an idea. He suggested they each go off in a different direction for a time. "Let's part company," Abraham said. Abraham even let Lot have first choice of the land for his own herds.[3]

Abraham let Lot have first choice. And Lot was selfish. Lot chose the very best land, in the valley, and took his herds there.

Even though Lot took the best land, Abraham was satisfied. He knew he had done what was right. And

[1]When are you most likely to feel like Abraham's and Lot's herdsmen? How do you think they felt about each other when they were quarreling?

[2]Do you think quarreling made the men feel better or worse? Why? How do you usually feel when you've been quarreling with a friend (or brother or sister)? What do you think people can do to stop quarreling?

[3]Sometimes people need to part company for a while. Can you think of a time when deciding to play apart for a while would have helped you?

Abraham knew that God was pleased with him. God would take care of him, and be with him forever.[4]

Action Idea Play a variation of "What If . . . " with your children. Choose several common situations that stimulate quarreling around your house. Make the children a "panel of experts," and let the parents (or one parent and an older child) role play (spontaneously act out) one of these situations. Stop the role play, and let your children tell you how to solve the problem. Let them act out the solution they suggest, or tell you how to act it out.

[4]*If you gave a friend first choice of something you were quarreling about, and he took the thing you wanted, how would you feel? Would you rather have kept on quarreling?*

God Makes a Promise
Genesis 15:1–21

Do you think this man could become a father?

Background   This story is retold to pick up an emphasis given to the covenant in the New Testament Book of Hebrews: that God made His promise, and confirmed the promise by an oath (covenant) "so that, by two unchangeable things in which it is impossible for God to lie, we who have fled to take hold of the hope offered to us [in Jesus] may be greatly encouraged" (6:18). How good it is to know that you and I—and our children—have a God who cannot lie. His words to us are sure, and His promises will never fail. It is because of God's character as a completely trustworthy person that we can trust Him so confidently.

38

Abraham was about seventy-five years old when God told him to leave his home and move to a new country. Abraham did what God told him. He took his wife, Sarah, and his herds and his cattle and the people who worked for him, and they traveled for weeks and weeks. Finally they came to the land of Palestine. They had arrived in the special land God said He would give to Abraham and to his children!

Abraham traveled over the land and had many adventures. But one thing Abraham didn't have. Abraham didn't have any children! How could Abraham inherit the land for his family if he didn't *have* any family?[1]

We know that Abraham was very unhappy about not having children. Once when God promised to reward Abraham, Abraham complained to God. "O Lord," Abraham complained, "what can you give me, since I remain childless?" Nothing seemed as important to Abraham as the children he was too old to have.

But God spoke to Abraham and made a promise. "You will have a son of your own." God told Abraham to look up into the night sky. "See if you can count the stars."

Abraham looked up. The sky was filled with all the stars we can see today—far more than anyone could ever count.

And then God said something amazing to Abraham. "You will have a son, and he will have children. Your family will become so large that it will be impossible to count them!"[2]

The Bible tells us, "Abraham did believe God."

Abraham was sure that God was powerful enough to make Abraham able to have a son. Most of all, Abraham was sure that God would never lie. Abraham trusted God, and God was pleased with Abraham.[3]

Let's thank God that He is someone we can always trust. And let's ask God to help us be like Him, so others will be able to trust us, too.

Action Idea To stress the trustworthiness of God, let your child do his own "promise search." Third-graders

[1] *Do you know anyone who is seventy-five or eighty years old? They're too old to be mothers or fathers; they're old enough to be grandfathers and great-grandfathers. Do you think Abraham felt happy being so old and not having any children?*

[2] *How do you think Abraham felt when he heard God say that? Abraham was very old. Do you think it was hard or easy for Abraham to believe what God said about him still having children? Why?*

[3] *Can you think of someone who has told you a lie, and you found out about it later? How did that make you feel about that person? Will it be easy to trust him again, or not? Why?*

are old enough for a Bible of their own, and can find promises there, or in your Sunday school literature. Or suggest that your child select one of the following four verses: Hebrews 13:5; Zechariah 8:8; Jeremiah 33:11; Isaiah 41:10.

Your child can then make a promise poster for his or her own room, or for the family.

Look at the sky on a clear night. You can see over 3,000 stars. But scientists looking through telescopes have found *millions* of stars! Look at the stars through a little telescope or a pair of binoculars. How many more stars can you see? The stars remind us that God is faithful. God keeps His promises.

Abraham Talks to God About Sodom
Genesis 18:16–33

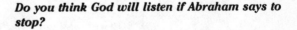

Do you think God will listen if Abraham says to stop?

Background   This simple Genesis story not only teaches us much about the compassion of God, but also provides a model which helps parents and children talk through family issues which may be in dispute.

The passage gives us even more confidence in prayer. God is never angry when we come to Him to express our concerns as well as our needs, our doubts as well as our praise.

One day the Lord told Abraham something He was about to do. One of the cities in Palestine, called Sodom, was a very wicked city. "Their sin is terrible," God told Abraham. And God told Abraham He was going to look over the city of Sodom one more time—and then destroy it.

Abraham stood there and thought about what God said. He thought very hard, and his brow wrinkled. He wanted to say something to God. But Abraham wasn't sure if he should. You see, Abraham didn't think what God was planning was fair. But how could Abraham say something like that to God?[1]

Abraham felt worried. Would God be angry if Abraham spoke up? Well, Abraham knew God loved him. So finally Abraham went up to the Lord and he blurted out what he was thinking.

"God, what if there are fifty good people in that wicked city? Lord, that wouldn't be fair! You wouldn't kill the good people with the sinners, would You? I think You ought to let everyone live if there are just fifty good people there."[2]

Even though Abraham seemed to accuse God of being unfair, God didn't get angry. Instead He told Abraham, "If I find fifty good people there, I won't destroy the city."

But Abraham still wasn't happy. "Lord, please don't be angry with me, now," Abraham said. "But what if there are only forty-five good people there? Will You destroy the whole city because there are five less than fifty?"

God was very patient. "If I find forty-five good people there," God promised, "I will not destroy the city."

Abraham still wasn't satisfied. He kept right on talking. Abraham asked what about forty people? And thirty? And twenty? And ten?[3]

God knew that Abraham was really worried about any good people in Sodom. God cared about any good people there too. So God was very patient. He didn't get angry at Abraham, but listened to Abraham carefully.

[1] Have you ever wanted to tell your parents or a teacher you think something they're going to do isn't fair? Can you tell us about it? (Share an experience from your own childhood, or a similar experience as an adult.) Is it easy or hard for you to tell an adult you don't think something they're doing is fair? Why? How do you think Abraham felt? Do you think he'll talk to God about it or not? Why?

[2] How do you suppose God felt when Abraham said He wasn't being fair? What do you think God will probably do?

[3] Do you think it's good if children keep on talking with their parents when they don't think something is fair? Why do you suppose God kept listening to Abraham? (You might note that Abraham was really worried and upset. Arguing just to argue is one thing. When a child, or person like Abraham really cares, then it's good for parents and others to be patient.)

Finally Abraham was satisfied. God promised not to destroy the city if even ten good people lived there.

Talking it out with God made Abraham feel much better. And God had listened patiently, and had not been angry at all.[4]

> **Action Idea** Make "listening" and "politeness" certificates.
>
> *Listening Certificate.* "Good for ten minutes of careful listening. To be presented when I have a problem, or feelings that are important to me, that I want to talk about. To be honored by mom (or dad) as soon as possible."
>
> *Politeness Certificate.* "Good for stopping and thinking, and then starting to talk again. To be presented when I feel I should be talked to with more respect. To be honored by (child's name) as soon as possible."

[4]*What are some of the things you like to talk out with mom or dad? Things that don't seem fair, or that you worry about? (Assure your child that you want to be like God, to listen and help. Explain too that it helps adults listen when children are respectful, as Abraham was with God.)*

Close in prayer, asking God to help you parents be as fair as He is, and to listen to your children when they want to talk about something important to them.

Ishmael Is Sent Away From Home

Genesis 16, 21

Who is saddest when a dad and his boy can't live together anymore?

Background The breakdown of a family always involves hurt and tragedy. Even when both parents are convinced a divorce is necessary, the children will suffer. It is vital then that we be particularly sensitive to the children and to their feelings at this crucial, stressful juncture of their lives.

The story of Abraham and his son Ishmael has many parallels to the plight of divorcing parents today. Retelling this Bible story may help a child who has experienced the divorce of his parents. You can help him express and explore his feelings, and assure him that he is still important to God.

In Abraham's day, people thought it was all right for a man to have more than one wife. When Abraham's wife Sarah did not have any children, she wanted Abraham to have another wife so Sarah could have children around her home.

But when Abraham did what Sarah wanted, Sarah wasn't happy. When a boy was born, and named Ishmael, Sarah was even angry. She didn't like Ishmael and she didn't like Ishmael's mother, either.[1]

Abraham's family lived together unhappily for many years. No one was very happy. But Abraham loved his son Ishmael very much. And Ishmael loved his father.

Then, when Ishmael was about twelve years old, Abraham's first wife Sarah had a baby boy too. She named him Isaac. Sarah loved Isaac, and she didn't like it when Abraham played with Ishmael. Sometimes Ishmael teased Isaac, and Sarah didn't like that either.

Finally Sarah said to Abraham, "You've got to get rid of Ishmael and his mother. Send them away."[2]

Well, Abraham was very upset. How could he ever send Ishmael away! Why, Abraham loved Ishmael. Probably Abraham felt angry at Sarah for suggesting he send Ishmael away.

Then God spoke to Abraham. "Do what Sarah says this time. Send Ishmael away." It seemed hard. But God made a promise. God promised to take care of Ishmael Himself. "I will make him a great people (nation)," God promised, "because he is your son." The next morning Abraham did what God told him. He sent Ishmael and his mother away.[3]

Abraham felt very sad. He loved his boy, and he didn't want him to be gone.[4]

Sometimes hard things happen to people. The hard things don't mean that we're not loved. They don't mean that we're being punished, or that we've done anything wrong. Sometimes hard things just happen, like they did for Abraham and Ishmael. But Abraham felt good about one thing. God would take care of Ishmael, even if Abraham could not. When bad things happen we need

[1] *Do you think it's hard or easy for people to live together in the same home when they don't like each other? How do you think people in that kind of family feel? How do you think the children feel?*

[2] *Since Abraham loved Ishmael very much, did he want to send Ishmael away from him? What do you suppose Ishmael felt and did?*

[3] *How do you suppose Ishmael felt when he was sent away? Was he angry? Sad? Did he think it was his fault, or did Ishmael blame someone else?*

[4] *Do you think your father (mother) felt anything like Abraham did when the judge decided you couldn't live with him anymore? How did you feel about being sent away?*

to remember that God still loves us. God will take care of us, whatever happens. God will never leave us alone.

Action Idea If your child has shared thoughts and feelings through the telling of this story, help him express those same feelings to God in prayer. Be ready to talk when he or she brings the subject up again. It is important for a child to talk through his anxieties and other feelings, and the subject may come up again and again.

Jacob's Dream
Genesis 28:10–22

Is it frightening to be alone in the dark?

Background Nighttime fears are common in younger children, as are frightening dreams. They need reassurance that it's all right to be frightened. And they need reassurance that their fears are groundless. God, who is more real than any nightmare, is with us even in the dark.

In this retelling of the story of Jacob's dream, much of the background is left out. This is to help your child of six to eight (more likely to fear the dark and to have nightmares than are older children) focus on the specific issues of darkness and dreams.

[1]How do you suppose you'd feel if you had to sleep outside alone in the dark? Jacob was grown up. But do you think he felt a little afraid? (Tell of a time as an adult when you felt anxious or afraid.)

[2]Do you remember any of your dreams? What's the best dream you ever had? What is the most frightening dream you ever had? (Share a nightmare of your own, and tell how you felt when you woke up.)

[3]What helps you most when you wake up from a dream and feel afraid?

[4]How would you feel at night if God promised you what He promised Jacob: "I am with you and will watch over you wherever you go"? It's not wrong to be afraid. But it helps when we're afraid to remember that God is with us, and that God is watching over us.

Jacob, one of God's own people, was on a journey. Jacob traveled all day, hurrying across an empty land. There were no towns or people where Jacob walked. How Jacob must have rushed, walking faster and faster, hoping to find someplace where he could stay at night.

Even though Jacob hurried, the sun seemed to hurry more. The sun kept on going down. It got lower and lower and lower. Finally Jacob knew. He was going to have to sleep out all night, in the dark, alone.[1]

We don't know just how Jacob felt there in the dark. But finally he used a stone for a pillow, and fell asleep. And when he was asleep, Jacob had a dream![2]

In Jacob's dream, he saw a great stairway. Its bottom rested on the earth, but its top seemed to reach all the way up to heaven. Looking carefully, Jacob saw God's angels going up and down the stairs.

And there, at the top, Jacob saw a figure he knew must be the Lord! The figure spoke to him. "I am the God of your grandfather Abraham and your father Isaac," God said. Then God made Jacob a promise. "I am with you and will watch over you wherever you go."

When Jacob woke up, he remembered his dream. Even though it was a good dream, Jacob felt afraid. Only later would Jacob remember God's promise to him.[3]

When morning came, Jacob thought and thought about his dream. Then he remembered what God had said to him. He remembered God's promise. "Since God will be with me and watch over me," Jacob said, "the Lord will be my God forever."

Then Jacob gave the place where he had slept a special name. He called it "Bethel," which means "God's house." Jacob would always remember that night. From then on Jacob knew God was always with him, to watch over him.[4]

Action Idea The best way to help our children with nighttime fears or nightmares is to be there when they need us, and to share calmly our own assurance that God is with them. This reality is not likely to sink in immediately. But with calm and loving repetition, the message of God's presence *will* take root. Our children's fears will gradually be quieted by the Lord.

You may also want to suggest your child set up his or her own "Bethel" reminder. Let him select several stones and glue them together to make a pillar, or pyramid (cf. Gen. 28:18). The stone pillar can be glued to a construction paper base, and the verse "I am with you and will watch over you" (Gen. 28:15) printed on it.

Joseph and His Brothers
Genesis 37

How would you feel if your brother or sister got some great new jacket—and you got nothing?

Background Reading in Genesis 37 we see the folly of the favoritism Jacob showed his youngest son. We also see the insensitivity of Joseph. He apparently took no wrongful pride in his privilege, but he did not seem to realize how hurt and jealous his brothers were. Surely telling them of a dream in which he saw himself exalted over them and his parents was woefully insensitive. But the folly of Jacob, and the insensitivity of young Joseph, were no excuse for the brothers' behavior. They nursed their jealousy and anger, and finally plotted against their younger brother. Their acts of sin were completely unjustified, no matter what their complaint.

50

Families aren't always happy. Sometimes parents or children say things that hurt others. Or we do something that makes others upset. There's a story in the Bible about a family who did things that hurt each other too. While I tell the story, see if anything that happened in this Bible family has happened in our family.

The father of this family was named Jacob. He had eleven sons. His youngest son was named Joseph. Jacob loved Joseph very much. In fact, he did things that made Joseph's brothers think that Joseph was their father's favorite. So the brothers became very jealous. Then one day Jacob went out and bought a beautiful new set of clothes for Joseph. Jacob didn't get anything at all for his other sons![1]

Joseph's brothers were hurt when their father showed that Joseph was his favorite. And they were angry at Joseph. It wasn't really Joseph's fault. But his brothers began to hate Joseph. They wouldn't even speak a kind word to him.[2]

Joseph didn't seem to think about how his brothers felt. In fact, when Joseph had a dream, he did a very foolish thing. The dream was from God, and it promised that one day Joseph would be a great man. The dream promised that Joseph's whole family would bow down to him in respect. But instead of keeping the dream to himself, Joseph hurried right out and told the dream to his brothers. "Someday," he told them, "you and even my parents will bow to me in respect!"[3]

There may not have been anything Joseph could do to help his brothers feel better. But Joseph didn't need to rub it in by telling his dream. That only made Joseph's brothers hate him more.

But then Joseph's brothers did a terrible thing. They didn't just say mean things to Joseph. The brothers were taking care of sheep in distant fields. When Joseph came from home with a message, they grabbed their brother. They took the special robe Jacob had given Joseph and dipped it in sheep's blood. Then they sold

[1]*Have you ever felt that someone else was mom's or dad's favorite? How did you feel inside then? (It's appropriate if your child has told about an incident to apologize and to reassure him or her that you really do love him.)*

[2]*Why do you think the brothers were angry at Joseph? Have you ever felt angry at someone in the family because he or she seemed to be the favorite? Can you tell us about it?*

[3]*How do you think his brothers felt when Joseph told them his dream? Do you think Joseph cared about his brothers' feelings?*

51

4What are some things
we should never do, no
matter how angry we
are? (Talk about limits,
making sure physical
aggression is clearly off
limits to your boys and
girls as a way to
express anger or
jealousy.)

their brother Joseph to be a slave in Egypt. They told their father Joseph had been killed by wild animals.

It was one thing to be angry with Joseph, and to talk mean to him. That was bad enough. But to sell their brother to strangers was a very, very bad thing![4]

All the members of this family had been foolish and wrong. And now everyone was unhappy. Jacob, who had showed favoritism to Joseph, thought his son was dead.

Joseph, who hadn't thought about how his brothers felt and had just made them more jealous, was a slave in Egypt.

The brothers were sorry when they saw how unhappy Jacob was. And they must have felt guilty when they thought of the bad thing they had done to Joseph.

The way this family acted had now made them all feel miserable and sad.

But God loved Jacob and Joseph. And God loved the brothers too. In Egypt, Joseph became rich and famous. Years later when there was no rain, and food would not grow in Palestine where Jacob lived, the brothers came to Egypt looking for food. Joseph found them there, and Joseph was able to see to it that they had all the food they needed to eat. In fact, the whole family moved to Egypt, and Jacob saw his son Joseph again! Joseph forgave his brothers, and gave them all land to live on while they stayed in Egypt.

How much happier the family was then, when everyone forgave each other for their hurts. How good God was to help them love each other in the end.

When we're jealous or angry at members of our family, we want to remember this. God will help us forgive them. When we do, everyone will be much happier, because God's ways are the best ways for us all.

Action Idea Work with your children to develop "what to do" lists. Two lists you can develop are:

*What should I do if I feel hurt and jealous of my brother or sister?

*What should I do if I think my brother or sister is jealous or angry at me?

Joseph in Egypt
Genesis 39—41

How would you like to visit Egypt as a slave?

Background One source of a sense of self-confidence and achievement is the knowledge that we have made right choices, even when it was hard. This is a difficult lesson to learn. But it is an important one. As Jesus taught, faithfulness in small things prepares us for larger responsibilities (Matt. 25:23). Our boys and girls grow to healthy maturity by experiencing a series of situations in which they learn to make right choices—even when they are hard ones.

Joseph was a stranger in the land of Egypt. He was a slave. Joseph's family was many miles away. And Joseph was only seventeen years old!

Joseph must have felt lonely and helpless at times. What could a slave do? What would become of him? But even when Joseph felt sad and unhappy, he tried to do his best.

Joseph worked for a man named Potiphar (pot-i-far). Joseph worked hard for his master, and soon Potiphar began to trust Joseph. God was with Joseph, too, and Joseph was successful in whatever he did. Soon Potiphar put Joseph in charge of everything he owned. Joseph must have felt good about that. He tried to do the right thing even when he didn't feel happy, and God had helped him do well.[1]

Joseph must have felt as proud and satisfied as you do when you do something well. God had helped Joseph, even though he was still a slave.

But then a terrible thing happened. Potiphar's wife asked Joseph to do something he knew was wrong. Joseph refused. But his master's wife kept urging him. Again and again Joseph said no. "My master trusts me," Joseph said. "How could I do such a wicked thing and sin against God?"[2]

Usually when we do what is right, good things happen to us. But sometimes we do the right thing and something bad happens to us. Perhaps other people don't understand. Maybe our friends get angry at us. Or maybe we get blamed anyway.

Well, Joseph did the right thing. But Potiphar's wife went to her husband and accused Joseph of doing something wrong! Potiphar was very angry. He didn't listen to Joseph. Instead he had Joseph thrown into prison for life![3]

In the end, even though Joseph had felt hurt and upset to be in prison, God had a good reason for what happened. In prison Joseph met some officials of Egypt's king. Later, when the king of Egypt had a dream he couldn't understand, one official remembered that God

[1] What are some of the things you do well? What do you do that makes you feel good about yourself—things you're proud of? (Add several things your child is accomplishing that make you feel proud of him or her.)

[2] Are there times when you want to do something you know is wrong? (Tell about a temptation of your own when it's hard to do the right thing.)

[3] Have you ever done something you know is right, and something bad happened to you anyway? Tell us about it. How did you feel when that happened? Were you still glad you had done the right thing? Why, or why not?

had helped Joseph understand dreams. The king of Egypt called for Joseph, and Joseph explained the dream to the king. The king freed Joseph and made him a ruler of Egypt.

Joseph had kept on doing what is right, even when it was hard. And God rewarded Joseph in the end.[4]

> **Action Idea** The story of Joseph's experiences in Egypt is an exciting Bible narrative, covering chapters 39—41 in Genesis. Your children can be helped to know and identify with this great Old Testament saint, whose faith was so strong. Read one chapter together for three consecutive evenings or at meal times. Talk about Joseph's feelings at each stage of his adventure. And talk about how confidence in God helps us to choose right even if good things do not seem to result right away.

[4]*What do you suppose God has planned for you to do or be when you grow up? What would you like to be? When we choose to do what is right, even when it's hard, we're like Joseph. We are getting ready for the special future God has planned for us.*

TALKABLE STORIES FROM THE REST OF THE OLD TESTAMENT

Moses Returns to Egypt
Exodus 4:1–17

Where would a shy person be? Why?

Background Most children are familiar with the story of Moses. They know about his discovery in a basketboat by the princess of Egypt, and about his experience with the burning bush. They know about his contest with Pharaoh and the plagues. They have seen pictures of Moses, beard rippling in the breeze, standing on Sinai with the Ten Commandments given Israel by God. But Moses was not a self-confident man. In fact, Moses had the fears of all timid people and seems to have been painfully shy at the thought of returning to Egypt, to appear before God's people there.

In God's dialogue with the hesitant Moses, recorded in Exodus 3 and 4, your shy child can find encouragement. God does understand and will help him or her.

You remember the story of Moses and the burning bush, don't you? Yes, God spoke to Moses then. God told Moses to go back to Egypt, and free God's people from slavery.[1]

Moses didn't feel excited when he heard what God wanted him to do. Moses didn't even feel happy. Instead, Moses was worried and upset. He was afraid. What would the people think if Moses tried to talk to them about God?

So instead of saying, "Yes, Lord, I'm ready to go," Moses hesitated. "But God, what if they won't believe me?" Moses asked.[2]

God knew that Moses was shy about going back to Egypt. But Moses was the best person for the job God wanted to be done. God could help Moses be successful, even though Moses felt shy.

Then Moses asked, "What if they won't listen to me?" God gave Moses special powers to prove to the people back in Egypt that God had sent him. Moses' long shepherd's staff would turn into a snake when Moses threw it on the ground. And Moses could turn fresh water into blood. But Moses was still afraid. Sometimes even when we know we can do special things we still feel shy.

So Moses said to God, "O Lord, I've never been able to speak well. I talk slow, and sometimes I even stutter." Moses was so worried he'd seem foolish. Moses was worried that he wouldn't be able to speak up if he tried.[3]

God wasn't angry at Moses. Instead He reminded Moses of something important. "Who gave people mouths to speak with anyway?" (Of course, the Lord did!) And then God made Moses a promise. "Now go; I will help you speak and teach you what to say."

"I will be with you," God told him. "I will help you speak." But Moses still felt afraid. Moses was still shy, and he was still worried.

"O Lord," Moses said, "please send someone else to do it." When a person is shy, sometimes it is hard even if he or she knows God is there to help.

[1]How do you suppose Moses felt then? Would he be more frightened or excited? How do you suppose you would have felt if that had happened to you?

[2]Have you ever felt like Moses . . . kind of afraid and worried and upset when you have to talk in front of others? Why do you think speaking up is so hard for Moses and other people?

[3]What do you suppose God will say to Moses now? Do you think there is anything that can help Moses feel better? What helps you most when you feel shy or timid?

God was not happy with Moses. But God still wanted Moses for this special job. So to help Moses even more, God said that Moses' brother, Aaron, could go with him to help.

It was hard for Moses. But he did go back to Egypt as God told him to do. There God did help Moses as He had promised. God helped Moses, a very shy man, become one of our greatest Bible heroes.

Action Idea Shyness is very painful for children and for adults. And shyness doesn't just go away. There's no quick solution through advice ("Just speak up, dear") or urging ("Why not go next door and meet the new neighbors?"). Only time and a number of experiences with other children and adults will help your child feel more comfortable.

What this Bible story is designed to do is to provide the transforming gift of hope. Children, like you and me, need to be sure that God and others will be patient. They need to feel we are not discouraged with them. Your shy child may want to hear this Bible story often. As you tell it, avoid giving advice and avoid urging special action. Instead, let the encouraging message of Moses—a timid man who becomes a great leader—create confidence that God will help your boy or girl, too.

God's People Rebel
Numbers 13, 14

What might happen to people who disobey God?

Background The New Testament book of Hebrews returns to this incident, with warning. "Today, if you hear his voice, do not harden your hearts" (4:7). God had promised His Old Testament people a homeland in Palestine. God had freed them from slavery in Egypt and led them safely through the desert. Yet, when God commanded them to go into the Promised Land and to take it from the strong nations that lived there, Israel refused. Fearful, unwilling to trust God, they rebelled against His command.

The story highlights the importance of obedience and the dangers of disobedience. God did know what was best for His people. He wanted to bless them. But they refused to obey and suffered the tragic consequences.

"Good news! Good news!" That was what Caleb and Joshua shouted when they came back to the Israelite camp.

The Israelites were camped outside the land God had promised to give them. For years they had been slaves in Egypt. But God had sent Moses to be their leader. And God had rescued them from Egypt! God brought them safely to the edge of the Promised Land. Every day God gave them special food to eat, called manna. Now God told them to go in and take the land the Lord was ready to give them.

No wonder Caleb and Joshua cried out, "Good news!" They had gone to scout the new land. Now they were so excited! It was a wonderful land. The fields were rich, and the crops that grew there were the best Caleb and Joshua had ever seen.

But when Caleb and Joshua got back, they found other scouts had returned with bad news! The crops were rich. But the people who lived in that country were very strong. They had powerful armies, and they looked as tall as giants.

Caleb and Joshua were surprised. Yes, the people of the land were tall and strong. But God would certainly fight for His people. Caleb stood up and said to everyone, "We should go up and take possession of the land, for we can certainly do it!"[1]

God had told His people to take the land. God had promised He would be with them. But except for Moses and Aaron, and for Joshua and Caleb, everyone was afraid! "God just wants us to get killed in battle," some of the Israelites said. "Let's go back and be slaves in Egypt," others said. Before long, not one person there would obey God and go up to take the land.

Moses and Aaron were so upset they actually cried! Joshua and Caleb begged the people. "This is a wonderful land. God will give it to us if we only obey Him. Don't rebel against the Lord. Remember God is with us, and don't be afraid of their armies."

But the people of Israel wouldn't listen to them. They

[1]*How do you suppose God's people felt when Caleb told them to go up to the land and take it? Why do you suppose Caleb was so sure they could do it?*

²Why do you suppose the Israelites wouldn't trust God and obey Him? Can you think of times when it's hard for you to obey God? What do you usually do then?

refused to obey God. They became so angry at Moses and Aaron and Joshua and Caleb, who did want to obey God, that they even talked about killing them.[2]

God was very angry. The people who would not obey the Lord could never live in the Promised Land. Only when we trust God and obey Him can He give us the good things He wants us to have.

So the Israelites went back out into the desert. They traveled in the desert for thirty-eight years. Finally, when all the grown-ups who had rebelled against God died, their children went back to the Promised Land, just as God had promised.

When you and I obey God today, He is able to give us the good things He wants us to have. When we disobey, God will forgive us. But we may miss out on good things.

Action Idea From a map in the back of a family Bible, trace or draw an outline of the Promised Land. Cut out green construction paper to represent Palestine. Use yellow to represent desert all around its borders. Attach the map to a family bulletin board or corkboard.

With your six- to eight-year-olds, make up a list of ways they want to obey God. Use only the issues your children suggest. Then make up a small symbol for each issue, small enough to be glued to the head of a thumb tack. Let your child place tacks either inside the green Promised Land area (which shows he is obeying God), or in the yellow wilderness area (which shows he needs to begin to obey God).

Praise your children for their acts of obedience. And be available to talk about things they find hard to do.

The Death of Moses
Deuteronomy 32, 34

How do families feel when a grandparent dies?

Background A death in the family brings grief to children. And it raises questions. When adults refuse to talk with boys and girls about the death of loved ones, children are left alone to deal with their grief, their doubts, and their fears.

Because the death of loved ones is a time of unique stress for children and for adults, several stories in this book are related to dying.

This Bible story is about the death of an older adult, who has lived a full life.

Death brings stress to adults as well. We need God's help to enable us to express our grief to our children, and to help them with theirs. Together we can find our Lord's healing touch in the memory of God's goodness to our loved one, and in the assurance that one day we will be together again in the Lord.

Moses was very old now. His hair and his beard were white. He must have been tired. For many years Moses had worked hard, leading God's people, Israel. Moses had many hard times. He had good times too. And now, with Moses' work finished, everyone loved him. They all trusted Moses, and knew that Moses loved them.

God loved Moses too. Moses had been God's friend, and faithful to the Lord. But God knew it was time for Moses to die.

One day God told Moses that he was to die soon. We don't know how Moses felt. But Moses knew that God would be with him. So Moses wasn't afraid. I suppose Moses felt sad about leaving his people, because they were his family. In fact, Moses called everyone together to say good-bye. Moses blessed them and promised them God's best.

And then it was time.

Alone, Moses began to climb up into the hills. He climbed on, up toward the top of Mount Nebo. But Moses was not really alone. God was with him.

God let Moses look out from the top of Mount Nebo. Across the river, in the valley, Moses could see the land God had promised to His people. Moses knew that soon the family he was leaving would be there, in the Promised Land. Moses must have been happy about that. Moses would miss his people. And they would miss Moses. But Moses knew that God would take care of the people he left behind.

Moses died then.

He was an old man.

Back in the camp all the people of Israel wept and cried. They had loved Moses very much. For thirty days they mourned Moses, and their hearts hurt with grief.[1]

But finally the time of grieving and weeping came to an end. God helped to heal their hurt. Then they could remember Moses and talk about Moses without feeling quite so sad.[2]

God buried Moses' body there on the mountain. Moses was gone. But God would be with Moses' friends and loved ones always. One day, when Moses' friends grew old and they died too, they would be with Moses again. And with the Lord.

Action Ideas This story is without *talkables,* for a reason. This may be a story you'll want to tell your children soon after the death of a beloved grandparent or other older family friend. It may not be wise to encourage children to talk at first. But your children do need to hear your voice speaking, reading with mixed sorrow and hope about dying.

You will probably find that your child will ask for the story of Moses' death often in the days and weeks following a grandparent's death. Soon your boy or girl may be ready to talk about grandpa or grandma. When they are ready, insert the following talkables when you tell the story, where indicated by numbers.

[1]It's all right to be sad when someone we love dies. We know we'll miss that person and we hurt inside. How did you feel when grandpa (grandma) died? (Share your own feelings, and describe them as fully as you can.) Even though we know God is with our grandpa (grandma), we miss him and are very sad.

[2]What happy things do you think Moses' people remembered about him? What happy things do you remember about grandpa (grandma)? Grandpa (grandma) was a very special person to us. Let's thank God for him and the good times we remember.

In time you may want to undertake a special project together which can be very healing. Make a "Happy Memories Book," using family pictures and your child's written accounts of good times with the loved one who has died.

Rahab's Choice
Joshua 2

Color the ribbon red for Rahab's faith.

Background Rahab was a citizen of Jericho in the time of Israel's conquest. She, and all her people, had heard of Israel and feared Israel's God. No one in Jericho seems to have doubted the stories of God's power. Yet their reaction was one of antagonism and terror. They locked themselves inside their walled city, and waited, trembling.

Only Rahab was willing to trust that God would protect her. Rahab's belief that God is real and powerful was translated into faith: she was willing to actually trust herself to the Lord.

Young children have difficulty understanding Bible terms like "faith" and "trust." Of course they "believe in God." So the story of Rahab will help them sense the underlying meaning of Christian, saving faith. Children will begin to see that faith in God means trusting oneself to Him.

"Israel is coming! Israel is coming!"
The soldiers of Jericho ran to close the great gates set in Jericho's giant stone wall.

Everyone else in the city ran to hide in their houses. They knew all about Israel. They had heard stories of Israel's God. They knew the Lord had parted the waters of the Red Sea, and rescued Israel from slavery in Egypt. They knew God fought for His people, so Israel won its wars. Everyone in the city was terrified. They had no doubt at all that the Lord is God of heaven and earth.

But even though the people of Jericho knew how great God is, they decided to fight God's people.[1]

Everybody in Jericho was ready to fight God's people—everybody except one person. That person was a woman named Rahab. When the gates of the city were closed, two Israelites, who had come to see Jericho, were inside the city. Now the soldiers were looking for the two Israelites to kill them. But the two Israelites were inside Rahab's house, and Rahab was talking to them.

"We have all heard about the Lord," Rahab said. "The people of Jericho want to kill you. But I will hide you. Only promise me that when you take the city, I and my family can become one of you. I want to trust myself to you and your God."[2]

So the men promised Rahab. When God's people took the city of Jericho, the enemy would be killed, but Rahab and her family would be safe. "Only hang a red ribbon outside your window," the scouts told her. "Then we'll know not to hurt you." Later that night Rahab helped the two Israelite scouts escape over the city wall.

Finally the Israelites attacked Jericho. God helped them, just as the people of Jericho feared. The city was destroyed and all the people in the city were killed.

All except Rahab and her family.

Rahab was safe. She became one of God's people. And Rahab trusted the Lord all her life.

[1] *Why do you suppose the people of Jericho wanted to fight? How do you think they felt? What do you think they might have done instead of fighting?*

[2] *God loves all people. But in the whole city, where everyone knew who God was, only Rahab was willing to trust herself to God. (You may want to share if you remember a special time when you trusted yourself to the Lord.) God will accept anyone who decides to trust Him, and welcome that person into God's family.*

Action Idea Children in many Christian homes grow up knowing about Jesus, secure in His love as part of their first memories. They do trust themselves to the Lord, and not just know about Him.

Yet sometimes our children are troubled by a sense of sin and guilt. At such times, the story of Rahab can lend comfort, and even stimulate the decision which brings peace with God (Rom. 5:1).

Remind your child that Rahab was one of the enemies of God. But when Rahab was willing to trust herself to God, God accepted her and saved her.

Jesus came and died for us that we might be forgiven for our sins, and become members of God's family. No one who trusts himself to Jesus will ever be turned away. We have Jesus' own promise, in John 6:37: "Whoever comes to me I will never drive away."

Jericho Taken

Joshua 5, 6

Would you feel safe behind these walls?

Background Jericho was an object lesson for Israel. Israel must learn that obedience, even to instructions which must have seemed foolish, brings victory. Reading the story today as it is recorded in the Book of Joshua reminds us of this truth. God can be trusted to know and do what is best. Because He understands reality better than we, we are wise to obey.

The story of Jericho is one of the most familiar of Bible stories. To add interest to the familiar, and to help your children consider the lesson intended, the story is retold here in "correctable" form. That is, you will tell the story wrong, and let your boy or girl correct you when the story wanders from the text.

71

W̲e've got *to take the city of Jericho,* Joshua was thinking. Joshua was the leader of God's people Israel. It was Joshua's job to plan the attack on the land God promised them. God would give Israel the land. But Israel would have to fight.

But how could Israel take Jericho? Jericho was a strong city, with great, high stone walls.

Joshua stood in the valley and looked up at the walled city. Well, there was only one thing the Israelite army could do. They would have to climb those walls, and fight the men who stood at the top to shoot at them with arrows and to throw down great stones.

Joshua went back to the Israelite camp and gave his orders. "Start making ladders, men," Joshua said.[1]

No one had ever heard of attacking a city by just walking around it. But the people of Israel did what God said. They must have wondered that first day as they walked silently around Jericho and returned to camp. The people of Israel probably felt foolish the second day. By the third day, they might have been embarrassed.

At first the people of Jericho had been frightened of Israel. They stood terrified on the walls, and watched Israel march up to their city. But all the Israelites did was walk around the city, and go back to their camp. The second day when the Israelites marched up again, the army of Jericho must have thought, *O my. This time they'll attack and we'll all be killed.* But Israel didn't attack. They just walked silently around the city again! The third day someone on the city wall probably jeered at them.

"Go on back home," one may have yelled. "Marching can't hurt us."

On the fourth day, all the people of Israel must have been really angry. They probably felt even more foolish, just marching around the city. Maybe that's why the people of Israel decided not to wait for seven days. They were so angry that on the fourth day they started

[1] What? That's not what happened! What do you remember? (Let your child tell of Joshua's meeting with the angel of the Lord, and recall God's instructions.

to shout and yell without waiting for Joshua's command.[2]

Well, you're right. The people of Israel didn't yell on the fourth day. Instead they did just what God told them to do. They marched in complete silence for six days. They probably didn't understand God. They knew if He told them something, it was best for them to do it. We know God loves us and wants the best for us. So we do what He says.[3]

Finally, on the seventh day, the people of Israel marched around the city seven times. Then the trumpets blew. Everyone shouted, and the walls of Jericho fell down![4]

> *Action Idea* Make a list of family rules, and of Bible commands or moral precepts. Talk about the reasons for each. You'll find that boys and girls will understand your explanation for some rules, but they will not really grasp the rationale. Explain that when children and adults don't understand why God says "Yes" or "No," we have to be like the people of Israel at Jericho. We trust God to know what is best, so we obey Him even when we don't understand.

[2]*What? I've got that wrong? Well, what did happen then? (Let your child tell the story as it happened.)*

[3]*Has anyone ever ridiculed you for doing something mom or dad have told you, or something you think pleases God? (Most children have been teased by others for wanting to go home when mom told them, or not cheating, or not throwing stones at passing cars, and so on.) How did you feel then? What did you do?*

[4]*Do you think the walls would have fallen down if the people hadn't obeyed? What do you suppose God wants us to learn from this Bible story?*

Gideon Throws Down a Pagan Altar
Judges 6

Do you have to feel strong to do something very brave?

Background Gideon is another of the Bible's reluctant heroes. Gideon saw himself as the least important member of an insignificant family in Israel (6:15). Gideon was not even sure of God's ability to help His people.

Many boys and girls have an image of themselves that matches Gideon's. They do not see themselves as able or as significant. Their doubts about themselves may be expressed as shyness or timidity, or as an unwillingness to try new experiences.

In time, with success experiences, hesitant and uncertain children can gain confidence and overcome their timidity. But in order to risk trying, children and adults need to have some basis for hope. The story of Gideon will help shy children develop that hope.

Gideon looked around fearfully.

He looked to the left. He looked to the right. Gideon looked behind him too. Only then did he bend over to beat the grains of wheat out of the straw. Gideon was hiding as he worked because he was afraid the Midianites would see him and steal his family's food.

Gideon, like most Israelites then, felt weak and afraid. He wanted to hide, because he knew there was nothing he was able to do that could help.[1]

Gideon knew he wasn't as strong as some. Gideon wasn't popular like some others. Gideon's family wasn't rich or famous. So you can imagine how surprised Gideon was when an angel appeared to him as he was working, and said to him, "The Lord is with you, Mighty Warrior."

Mighty Warrior! Gideon almost laughed. But the angel said, "Go in the strength you have and save Israel from Midian."

"But Lord," Gideon said. "How can *I* save Israel? My clan is the weakest in our state, and I'm the least important in my family."[2]

Gideon felt much too weak and helpless to be a leader.

But when the Lord told Gideon to tear down his family's altar, where the people of his town worshiped an idol instead of the Lord, Gideon did try. He was afraid to do it in the daytime. So Gideon snuck out at night to destroy the idol and its altar.[3]

Later Gideon prayed to the Lord. "Lord," Gideon said, "please don't be angry. But if You really plan to use me to save my country, I'll put this sheepskin on the ground. Tomorrow if it is wet with dew and the ground is dry, I'll know You are with me."

The next morning, the sheepskin was wet and the ground was dry, just as Gideon had asked.

But Gideon still didn't feel confident. He still felt weak and afraid. So Gideon talked to God again. "Lord, please don't be angry. But if You plan to use me to save my

[1]*Have you ever felt like Gideon: weak, and afraid, and helpless? Do you like those feelings? When are you most likely to feel that way?*

[2]*Suppose the Lord called you a "mighty warrior." How would you feel? Do you ever feel like Gideon must have felt when you're asked to do things—like play games, or get ready for a test, or meet new people?*

[3]*Why do you think Gideon did it at night? Do you suppose it was all right to obey God that way, instead of marching bravely out in the daytime? We don't have to do something perfectly the first time. Being willing to try when we're afraid is very important, and pleases God.*

country, tonight make the ground wet and the sheepskin dry."

The next morning, the sheepskin was dry and the
ground was wet. God hadn't been upset with Gideon.
God knew that Gideon needed encouragement to feel
strong and able.

God wasn't in a hurry. God would help Gideon grow.
The time would come when Gideon wouldn't be timid
or afraid any more.

And you know, God was right about Gideon. God did
help Gideon. And because Gideon kept on trying even
when he was frightened, Gideon did become a great
leader. The Midianite enemies were driven out. And all
Gideon's life he was God's man to protect the people of
Israel from their enemies.

> *Action Idea* You can read the whole story of Gideon
> in three installments at mealtimes or bedtimes (Judges
> 6, 7, and 8). Older children may enjoy making a large
> chart of Gideon's life. Use graph paper, and draw ups
> and downs. For instance, an "up" would be when
> Gideon tore down the altar, a "down" when he hid af-
> terward.
>
> This chart can be helpful in a number of ways. Talk
> about the length of time it took for Gideon to become
> confident. Talk about Gideon's feelings at each "up"
> and "down" point. Talk about the trust in God that
> enabled Gideon to keep on trying even when he didn't
> feel strong and confident. When we trust God and keep
> on trying, we grow too. We become the kind of person
> we want to be.

Ruth Leaves Home
Ruth

Why is it easier to move when our family is going with us?

Background   Moving is a time of great stress for children from nine to eleven. It means leaving friends and the comfort of familiar sights, and the house in which they feel they belong. It's no wonder that getting ready to move may bring sadness and anxiety to boys and girls.

In another Bible story children were encouraged to think of moving as an adventure, and promised that God would be with them in their new home. In this story of Ruth, another emphasis is added. "Home" to Ruth was not to be found in a place, but in her relationship with an older woman she had grown to love.

One of the greatest comforts a child facing a move can experience is the assurance that, wherever the family moves, the family will still be together. We may leave familiar places behind us. But we will not leave the people we love most.

"Ruth, I have something to tell you."

Ruth looked up. Her mother-in-law, Naomi, seemed so serious. Ruth knew that Naomi had been quiet the last few days, as if she were thinking hard.

Ruth sat down near Naomi.

"All right, mother-in-law. I'm listening."

Naomi looked uncomfortable and a little unhappy. But she began to talk. "Ruth," Naomi said, "you know how my husband and I moved here years ago from Bethlehem."

Ruth nodded.

"My husband and I and our sons settled down here. And you met and married my boy. Then both your husband and my husband died."

Ruth nodded again. How hard it had been when the men of the family died and left Naomi alone, with only daughters-in-law to be with her.

Naomi took a deep breath. "Ruth, I've decided to move back to Bethlehem, in the land of Israel. You have been very good to me. And I am going to miss you. But I feel I have to move."[1]

Ruth thought for a moment.

And then she said, "Naomi, I'm coming with you!"

Naomi hugged her. She loved Ruth very much. But she shook her head sadly. "You're still young, Ruth. You should stay here and get married again. Back in my country, Israel, you would be a foreigner, and it might be hard to find a husband."

But Ruth just shook her head. She loved her mother-in-law, Naomi. She didn't want to think of Naomi being alone. So Ruth gave Naomi a big hug back. "Don't ask me to leave you," Ruth said. "Where you go I will go, and where you stay, I will stay. Your people will be my people and your God, my God." When Naomi realized Ruth was determined to go with her, Naomi stopped urging Ruth to stay.[2]

When the day came, Ruth and Naomi set out together for the land of Israel. In time the people of Bethlehem noticed what a good person Ruth was. Finally, she mar-

[1] *How do you think Ruth felt when Naomi told her she planned to move? What do you think was hardest about the plan for Ruth? (Share some of the things about the move that are hard for you too.)*

[2] *How do you suppose Naomi felt when she realized she wouldn't have to move alone? Why do you think that made moving easier? One of the things that helps me with moving is that our family will be together.*

ried a man named Boaz, and had a baby. How happy Naomi was then. Ruth still loved her mother-in-law. And now at last Naomi was a grandmother.

The family was still together.

And the new land, Israel, was home for them all.

Action Idea   Plan ahead ways that you can help each other prepare for the move, and how you can help when you arrive. In the process talk about the things that concern or worry each of you. If the children worry about how to make new friends, plan how you will help them meet new boys and girls. Maybe you can promise a party for neighborhood children when you move in. If you are worried about misplacing items, let your children work up a check-list and help you keep track of special treasures.

Whatever concerns are expressed by any family member, see if together you can work out ways to help each other meet the expressed need.

Samuel Listens to God
1 Samuel 3

How do we know someone is listening?

Background It's hard for children to listen to each other. And it's hard for us to listen to our boys and girls.

The familiar Bible story of the boy Samuel, usually told to children of three and four, has very different implications when we look at it from the unique standpoint of its listening subtheme.

This Bible story teaches us the importance of being responsive to God. But in it we also see the importance of listening in every interpersonal relationship. As told here, for the six- to eight-year-old, this Bible story is helpful for training your children to listen to each other carefully and well.

"**S**amuel! Samuel!" called Eli, the priest of Israel. "Here I am," answered Samuel, running to Eli. "Samuel," said Eli, "it's getting late. Time to go to bed."

Samuel walked back to the tent-church where he lived and helped, and crawled into his bed. *I'm glad God chose me to live here with Eli,* Samuel thought.

Eli was getting very old, and a strong eight-year-old like Samuel was able to help in many ways. *Maybe,* Samuel may have thought as he drifted off to sleep, *maybe God will want me to be a priest and help people worship Him. I'll want to listen very carefully to all the things Eli teaches me.*

Soon Samuel lay down to sleep. Samuel's eyes were closed, and he had just drifted off when . . . suddenly . . . he heard a voice calling, "Samuel! Samuel!"

Samuel sat up straight. Then he jumped out of bed and ran to Eli. "Here I am, Eli. What do you want?"

Eli looked surprised. "I didn't call you, Samuel," he said. "Go back to bed."

Samuel was sure he'd been called. But he went back to bed. Samuel snuggled down and pulled up his blankets. And then he heard the same voice calling again. "Samuel! Samuel!"

This time Samuel was sure. So he jumped up and hurried to Eli's room. "Here I am, Eli," Samuel said. "What do you want?"

Eli looked a little upset. "Samuel, I didn't call you. You'd better go back to bed and go to sleep."

Samuel was really puzzled now. But he walked back to his bed and sat down on it. Sure enough, he heard the voice again. "Samuel!" the voice called.

So Samuel got up a third time and went to Eli. Eli started to send Samuel back to bed, but then Eli stopped. "I wonder," Eli said to himself. "I wonder if God . . ."

So now Eli said to Samuel, "Boy, I think it was God's voice you heard. Go back to bed and if you hear the voice again, say this: 'Speak, Lord, for your servant is listening.' "

From that day on God did talk with Samuel. Samuel grew up to become God's messenger to the people of Israel. He spent his whole life listening to God, and telling God's people what the Lord said.[1]

Action Idea If your children need help learning to relate to friends or to other members of the family, the Samuel story can initiate a helpful "listening" exercise.

1. Divide family or friends into pairs. Take half the partners into another room. Instruct them to tell their partners about the best Christmas they ever had. Then return to the first room and instruct the partners to listen very carefully, because later each may have a chance to tell the partner's story to the others.

Bring the pairs together, and give them several minutes to talk and listen. Then ask the storytellers to nominate a "best listener." As individuals are suggested, ask what makes that person a good listener. Have the storytellers see if they can list what a good listener does to show that he or she is listening carefully. Write down the "good listener" traits.

2. Then take the other partners into the adjoining room. Tell them to think of the most exciting (fun) thing that has ever happened to them, to tell to their partners. While they are thinking of what to talk about, instruct the partners in the first room *not* to listen. They are not to walk away, or make noises. But they are to act as though they don't care what their partners are saying. They are to pretend they aren't listening.

After a minute or two, stop.

Ask the storytellers how they feel. What happened to make them feel that way?

Tell what you asked their listeners to do, and explain why. One way that we help people feel loved and important is to listen carefully to them. If we don't listen, they feel hurt or angry or unimportant. We can let people know we want to be friends and that we care about them just by listening.

Saul Is Chosen to Be King
1 Samuel 10

Who do you think would make the best king? Why?

Background   Israel's desire for a king was rooted in warped values. Israel wanted to be like the nations around them, and have a king who would go out to fight their battles for them (8:5, 19, 20). That desire was a rejection of what made Israel unique.

Older children are beginning to make important choices. Our children six through eight play with boys and girls who live nearby. Anyone reasonably polite and cooperative is considered a friend. But those nine through eleven look more carefully at other children, and select as friends those with traits they value. A look together at the story of Saul's choice as king can help your older boys and girls examine the values that are important to them in the choice of their friends.

[1] *Why do you think the people of Israel wanted to be like everyone else? Have you ever wanted to do something or have something because everyone else has it? That isn't really wrong. We all want to fit in with our friends. But can you think of any times when it might not be a good idea?*

[2] *Do you think the Israelites were wise to like Saul just because he was tall and handsome? Let's list some things that we would want if we were going to choose a king. (Make a list together.)*
Sometimes people pick friends because of how they look, or because they're big and strong. Let's make a list of things most people look for in a friend. (Make as long a list as you can, including important and superficial traits. When the list is complete, go through it together and decide which are good reasons for choosing a friend and bad reasons for choosing a friend.)

[3] *Do you suppose you'd want as a friend a jealous, angry person who didn't want to obey*

"But you don't *need* a king!" Samuel said angrily. "Don't you understand? *God* is Israel's king."

But all the people of Israel muttered and complained. "We want a king," the people insisted. "We want a king to lead us, so we can be like all the countries around us. They have kings. So we want a king too."

"Yes," someone else added. "When enemies attack us, our king can go out and fight for us."

"That's right!" everyone said. "We want a king!"

Later God spoke to Samuel. "Don't be upset, Samuel," the Lord told His prophet. "It's not you they have rejected. It's Me. Do what they want, but warn them solemnly that having a king is not wise."[1]

The thing that was wrong in Israel was that Israel wanted to be like everyone else so badly the nation turned away from God. It's all right to want to be like others who are good persons. It's foolish to want to be like people who do wrong things—people who don't care about pleasing God.

So God picked out just the kind of king the people of Israel would like. This man's name was Saul. He became Israel's first king. When Samuel pointed Saul out, and said that he should be king, almost everyone was pleased.

You see, Saul was very tall. He was good-looking too. He was a whole head taller than anyone else in Israel. *What a fine, big, good-looking fellow,* most people thought. *He'll make a fine king!*[2]

Later the people of Israel learned how foolish they were. Oh, Saul did help them some. He was a good fighter, and God helped Saul to win some battles.

But later Saul showed that he was a person who became jealous when others were praised. Saul was a person who didn't trust God enough to obey Him. He was a person who became angry at others, and he even killed some Israelites who made him angry. Saul was tall. And he was good-looking. But he wasn't really the kind of person Israel should have wanted for a king.[3]

Action Idea Our goal in exploring children's friendships is not to suggest that our boys and girls should isolate themselves from immature or difficult children. But it's important that older children develop their closest friendships with boys and girls whose basic values they share. It's good, when our boys and girls talk about new friends, that we encourage them to share things they like about the new acquaintance. In talking about things they like about their new friend, you can follow up on the themes introduced in this story, and focus your children's attention on deeper values rather than appearances.

God? Why, or why not? Who is your best friend now, and what is he (or she) like?

King Saul Is Afraid
1 Samuel 13, 15

Why would someone do something he is ashamed of and later tries to hide?

Background Saul's inner weaknesses are illustrated in two early incidents from his reign. On each occasion Saul disobeyed God because of what he imagined might happen if he obeyed. Saul's fears of the unknown overwhelmed his trust in the Lord. As a result this man was rejected and not permitted to establish a dynasty.

All of us are subject to fears of what we imagine might happen. Children, too, have many imaginary fears. Your goal in exploring the story of King Saul with your own boys and girls is not to make your children feel guilty about their fears, but rather to help them see that fears must not lead us to do wrong things.

Saul was king now, the leader of all Israel. It was exciting to be king. And Saul must have been proud. Saul was only thirty years old, but everyone was already telling him how great a man he was. Saul had led his people in one battle, and won it.

But then some new enemies attacked Israel. The Philistine army marched out to do battle.

Saul sent messengers throughout Israel. "Come help Saul fight the enemy," the messengers said. And Samuel, God's prophet, made a special promise to Saul. "Wait for me at Gilgal. Within seven days I will come, and will pray to the Lord that you will win a great victory."

So Saul and the men of Israel gathered at Gilgal. From there, looking over a valley, they could see the army of the Philistines on a hill across from them. It was such a big army! Why, the Philistines had three thousand chariots, like our tanks. And Israel didn't have any! There were so many Philistine soldiers no one could count them! King Saul looked around at his men. There weren't nearly as many soldiers of Israel. And the Israeli weapons weren't as good as those of the Philistines. But, Saul may have thought, *Samuel is coming. Samuel will pray for the Lord to help us.*

Samuel didn't come the first day. Samuel didn't come the second day. And as the Israelites kept looking at the Philistine army, many Israelites were afraid. Saul was afraid, too. Saul began to imagine what would happen if Israel lost!

The third and fourth day passed. Samuel still didn't come. Saul saw that some of the men of his army were sneaking away. He was losing soldiers! And Israel was already outnumbered!

The fifth day passed. The sixth day came. More of Saul's army was sneaking away to go home. How anxious and worried Saul felt now. How could Saul fight the Philistines with so few men? When the seventh day finally came, Saul kept looking and looking for Samuel. But Samuel didn't come in the morning. Samuel wasn't there by noon. The whole army of Israel was terrified now. Saul was the king. What could he do? As more and more of his army left, Saul could imagine what would happen. If Samuel didn't get here, why, he'd be left alone!

In Israel, only priests were allowed to present offerings to God. Saul was so afraid now that he decided not to wait for Samuel to come and make an offering. Saul started a fire on the altar, and made the offering himself. Just as Saul finished, Samuel came. Saul had been so afraid of what he imagined might happen. He had disobeyed God and done something he knew was wrong.[1]

That wasn't the only time Saul was afraid and disobeyed God. Later God sent Saul and Israel's army to fight a very wicked country. Saul was told by Samuel, "God wants you to destroy the whole country. Even their sheep and cattle are to be killed."

Saul attacked these enemies, and won. But then Saul took the king of that country captive. And Saul brought back all the healthy and strong sheep and cattle and calves and lambs God had ordered killed.

The next morning Samuel went to meet Saul.

Saul was very excited about Israel's victory. When Saul saw Samuel, he laughed and shouted a greeting: "God bless you!" And then Saul said, "I have carried out the Lord's instructions."

Samuel looked grim. "You did, did you? Then how come I can hear sheep bleating, and cattle lowing?"

Saul tried to make excuses. "I did what God said. I went on God's mission and destroyed the wicked enemy. It's just that the people wanted to keep the sheep and cattle. We, ah, plan to use them as an offering to the Lord."

Samuel was furious. "Does God want offerings, or does He want obedience? Why didn't you do what you knew was right?"

Finally Saul broke down and told Samuel what really happened. "I knew I was doing wrong. But, Samuel, I

[1] It's all right to be afraid. What's wrong is to let our fears of what might happen lead us to disobey. If you were to make up a story about a child your age who was like Saul, what would the story be about? What would the child be afraid of? What would he or she imagine might happen? What is the right thing he needs to do?

was afraid of what the people might do if I said no to them."[2]

Saul was very sorry afterward. But Samuel had a stern message for him from God. "Because you would not obey Me," the Lord had told Samuel, "I will find someone else to be king."

God needed a person who would trust and love Him enough to obey, even when he was afraid. Only that kind of person could be king and lead God's people Israel.

Action Idea Play "What If . . . " with your children using these two stories of Saul. Have your whole family participate.

Make up several possible endings that might have happened to Saul if he had not made the offering. For instance, Saul might have been left alone, and killed by a Philistine scouting party. Saul might have gotten into a fight with his own army, and had his tongue cut out, and so on.

Then make up as many possible good endings if Saul had obeyed. For instance, Saul was left with only 150 people, but God sent an earthquake and the whole Philistine army slid off the hill and crushed each other in the valley. Talk about which endings are most likely to happen, and why.

You can now use this approach to help your children analyze their own worries. First play "What If . . . ?" with situations your children may have described during story *talkables*. Then discuss other personal worries of theirs or your own in a "what if" way.

How good to know that with God committed to us, we can trust Him and choose to do right, despite what we fear might happen if we do.

[2]*How was this failure of Saul's like the first one? What was different? (In each case Saul imagined something that might happen. Instead of trusting God and obeying Him, Saul did something he knew was wrong. In this case Saul wasn't even afraid of an enemy. He was afraid of what his people, his friends, would think!)*

What do you usually do when you are afraid of what other people might think if you do what you believe is right?

David's Youth
1 Samuel 17:34–37

Would you trust a boy who protected his sheep from a bear?

Background Younger children may have persistent fears of imaginary terrors: of monsters and ghosts and, for those six to eight, of wild animals. In fact, fear of wild animals is the most common of young children's fears, even when there are no lions or tigers or bears within hundreds of miles of a child's home.

Such fears are normal, and should not be belittled. Instead, we can work quietly to build the child's base of confidence, trust, and security. This Bible story about the young David is told just for your six- through eight-year-olds.

90

David settled down on the hide under a tree. From the cool, grassy spot where he sat, David could see his sheep grazing in the meadow.

David was a musician as well as a shepherd. He wasn't a very tall boy. In fact, at sixteen David was smaller than most of his family. But David was strong. Living outdoors, and hiking over the fields with his sheep, had made David strong and healthy. His daily practice throwing stones with his sling had made David's arm strong, too.

But now David was sitting down, resting. David was playing songs on an instrument like a small guitar, and singing songs he made up himself. Many of David's songs were about God. Some songs were about the storms David saw in the mountains. Others told about the brooks and rivers and the animals he saw.

David had to stay awake in the afternoon, and watch because of bears and lions. Those wild animals were dangerous. And wild animals liked to eat sheep! David had to stay awake to protect his sheep. Usually, if David saw a bear or a lion, he'd pick up a stone, put it in his sling, and throw the hard stone at the wild animal. The stone hurt, and usually the lion or bear ran away.

Then one day something terrible happened. A big brown bear crept up on David's sheep. David threw stones with his sling. But the bear grabbed one of the sheep in his mouth and started to drag it away!

I've got to save my sheep, David thought. He probably felt afraid then. But David believed that God was able to save him from the claws of the bear. David jumped up and ran after the bear.

David carried a wooden staff, like other shepherds. When David got to the bear he beat it over the head with the staff. That hurt! The bear let loose of the sheep. David dragged the sheep right out of the bear's mouth, and started to carry it back to the flock.

My, that bear was angry! The sheep was to be its dinner! The bear growled and roared, and turned on David. But David had a knife too. When the bear at-

91

tacked, David jumped on the bear's back, grabbed its hair, and held on. The bear couldn't reach David to bite or claw him. But David could reach the bear. Holding onto the hair tightly with one hand, David stabbed the bear with his knife, again and again. He stabbed the bear until the bear died!

Then David realized what he had done, and he thanked God. "Lord," David said, "You have saved me from the bear. Thank You." David had been very brave! With God's help, David had been able to kill a dangerous wild animal.[1]

[1]*What part of the story do you like best? What do you think was David's best weapon against the bear? The sling? The staff? The knife? Let's thank God that He takes care of the people who trust Him, just as He took care of David.*

Action Idea This true story of David's victory over dangerous wild animals may stimulate your child to share his fears and feelings. If not, don't press him.

Instead, make a model with your child of David's "best weapon against the bear." A sling can be made with a piece of leather as a pocket, and two longer strings, one attached to each side. This biblical sling was swung around the head, one thong released, and the stone which fit into the pocket thus flung at the target. A staff can be formed from a tree branch in your back yard, or drawn on construction paper. The staff was a long stick with a hook at one end, used to lift sheep out of mountain crevasses into which they had fallen. A knife can also be outlined and cut from cardboard.

You may want to add a Bible verse to the chosen reminder: "The Lord who delivered . . . will deliver me" (1 Sam. 17:37). Let your child take his symbolic weapon into his bedroom, to remind him that with God's help even the young need not be afraid.

David and Goliath
1 Samuel 17:1–58

Who expects to win the fight between these two?

Background It's hard to think of a more familiar Bible story. Yet the tale of David and the giant Goliath remains a favorite of boys and girls.

This favorite Sunday school story, a feature of every curriculum, often asks children to identify the "giants" in their lives (their fears) and then remember that God can help us win if we confront our fears. Rather than take this approach, we want to help boys and girls sense that, because we can trust God, many of the things which seem to be dangers are not dangers at all.

King Saul sat slumped inside his tent. "Close that tent door," Saul yelled angrily at one of his soldiers.

The soldier jumped to obey. No one liked to be around King Saul when he was grumpy.

Of course, everyone knew why Saul was grumpy just now. It was ten in the morning, and that awful giant, Goliath, was going to march out and insult the army of Israel again.

It happened every morning. The two armies—the army of Israel and the army of the Philistines—were camped across from each other. But the Philistines had a soldier named Goliath who was nine feet tall! And he was strong. Why, his metal shirt alone weighed 125 pounds! His weapons were giant, too. And every day Goliath marched out into the valley between the two armies and yelled insults at the Israelites. Goliath dared the Israelites to send somebody out to fight him. Goliath called all of God's people cowards. But no matter how loudly he yelled, or what terrible insults he shouted, no one dared come out to fight. Goliath was just too big!

The biggest man in Israel, King Saul himself, sat inside his tent with the door closed so he couldn't see Goliath. You see, King Saul was afraid, too!

After days and days, a young shepherd boy visited the army to bring some food to his brothers, who were soldiers. You know the shepherd's name, don't you? Yes, it was David. Well, that morning David saw Goliath march down into the valley. David heard him insult God's people and challenge the Israeli army.

David looked around, expecting to see some soldiers jump up and run out to fight Goliath.

But no one moved. Instead, everybody muttered and looked around, or looked at the ground. Everyone seemed to be afraid! David was really surprised. He asked some nearby soldiers, "Who is this Philistine, to defy the armies of the living God?" Goliath was big, yes. But God surely was bigger. With God on Israel's side, David knew the giant didn't have a chance.

Someone told King Saul what David was saying. David

was brought to the king. "I'll go fight Goliath," David volunteered. "I've fought lions and bears to protect my sheep, and God has always protected me. God will protect me now from the giant."

Saul tried to give David Saul's own armor. But David was much smaller than Saul. The armor just wouldn't fit. So David went down into the valley, without any armor at all, to fight the nine-foot-tall Goliath.

How angry Goliath was when he saw David coming! Why, it was an insult! This wasn't a fighting man. It was only a boy! And instead of a sword, David carried only his wooden shepherd's staff! How Goliath howled!

But David called out to Goliath. "You come against me with your sword and spear and javelin, but I come against you in the name of the Lord, the God of Israel, whom you insulted. Today God will give me the victory, and I'll cut off your head. The whole world will know how great God is!"

David took a smooth stone he had picked up and put it in his sling. He ran toward the giant, swinging the sling around his head. David let the stone fly. Straight and hard, that stone flew right at Goliath and hit the giant in the forehead. Knocked out cold, Goliath fell flat. David ran to him, took Goliath's own sword, and cut off the giant's head!

David was right!

God's people don't have to be afraid of giants. God loves and helps His people. God's people don't have to be afraid at all.

> **Action Idea** It's enough for you and me, when we sense our children are afraid, to remark, "It's a good thing God is with you as He was with David when David fought Goliath." God made the difference then. He makes the same difference today.
>
> The sling David used was made of two leather strings and a leather pad. The stone was put in the pad. David held both strings and whirled the sling around over his head. David then let go of one string, and the stone flew out of the pad to hit his target.

Saul Is Jealous
1 Samuel 18

What is the worst thing about being jealous?

Background Jealousy is natural among children in any family. Children compete for their parents' attention and, in a sense, compete for love. You and I can't make jealousy go away by saying it is wrong. But we can reduce incidents which stimulate jealousy, or which might be misunderstood by children as parental favoritism.

We can also explore with older boys and girls something of the nature and the destructive impact of jealousy. In few biblical passages is the tragic impact of jealousy so clearly seen as in those which describe the declining years of King Saul.

After David killed Goliath, King Saul made David an officer in Israel's army. This pleased everyone. David was a hero, and naturally everyone cheered when David came along.

In fact, people even made up a song about David. It was a joyful song—one meant to be danced to. When the army came marching home after defeating the Philistines, the soldiers were met in every town by happy, dancing people, singing:

Saul has slain his thousands,
and David his tens of thousands![1]

Saul was very angry about the song. *I'm the king,* Saul thought. *And yet David gets more credit than I do.* From that moment Saul began to be jealous of David.

Saul was jealous because Saul saw how successful David was. Everything the king asked David to do, David did well. When David led the troops, the army of Israel always won. It was clear that God was helping David, and Saul remembered all the times that he had disobeyed the Lord. Saul knew inside that he wasn't as good as David. It was this that made Saul afraid and jealous.[2]

Poor Saul. He knew deep down that he was wrong. And David was always so helpful and loyal to him. But Saul just couldn't admit his own faults.

Saul became more and more miserable. He had times when he felt terribly depressed. Other times Saul flared up in anger. Saul even threw a spear at David while David was playing a harp to soothe his unhappy feelings. Jealousy is such a miserable thing. The person who is jealous will hurt others, and he is never happy himself.

For the rest of his life Saul was an angry, jealous, unhappy man.[3]

> ***Action Idea*** Tell this Bible story when you sense jealousy in one of your older boys or girls. Don't accuse them of Saul's kind of jealousy. It may be that something you have said or done unwisely made your child feel momentarily unloved. But it may be that some

[1]*How do you think Saul felt when he heard this song? Why would he feel like this? Saul was the tallest man in Israel. He should have fought Goliath himself, but Saul was afraid to. How do you think Saul felt about himself when he looked at David?*

[2]*What can a person do when he's angry and jealous because of something he knows is really his fault? What do you think would have happened if Saul went to God, confessed how he felt, and admitted the things he did wrong? Saul didn't do that. Instead, he continued to be angry and jealous and afraid all the time. Do you think you'd like that?*

[3]*What lessons do you think God wants us to learn from Saul's unhappiness? If you ever feel angry and jealous and it's because of something you've done wrong, what will you do?*

sense of personal guilt or failure is at the root of your child's feelings. If so, this story may encourage them to admit the problem and seek the healing, cleansing gift that is ours when we confess our sins to the Lord (see page 105).

Abigail Helps Calm David's Anger
1 Samuel 25

Would you be afraid to face an angry soldier?

Background What do children do with their anger? They're likely to feel angry, particularly when something happens to them they don't feel is fair. But there are very few ways we let children express anger. Yelling and shouting aren't popular with parents. Surely we can't let them express anger physically, by striking out or hitting others. And we do want to help them control their anger, learning to master it rather than having anger master them.

God encourages us to face the reality of our anger. The feelings are there: we can't deny them. But God also wants us to know that those angry feelings will change. God wants us to be able to work through our anger and find alternatives to the sins to which anger moves some.

King Saul had finally driven David away from his capital. In fact, Saul was determined to kill David. So David hid in the wildest part of Israel. David was joined there by other men who were loyal to him. But it was a hard life. David and his men were often hungry and cold.

Near where David and his men were hiding lived a rich man named Nabal, who owned thousands of goats and sheep. Those sheep grazed on the side of the mountain where David was in hiding. All the weeks that Nabal's shepherds had his flocks on the mountain, David and his men didn't take even one. In fact, David's men protected the shepherds and Nabal's sheep from any thieves and from wild animals.

So when it came time for the sheep to be sheared, and for Nabal's crops to be harvested, David thought it would be fair if the rich farmer gave some of the harvest to his men. David sent messengers to Nabal, and asked very politely.[1]

Nabal listened to the messengers. But Nabal didn't even ask his shepherds if what the messengers said was true. Instead Nabal insulted David. "Why should I take my bread and meat and share it with some lazy scoundrel?" And Nabal sent David's men away without any food.[2]

When David heard, he was furious. David's face turned red, and his blood pounded inside. In a terrible, angry voice, David shouted at his men.

"Put on your swords!" David shouted. And David started to rush down the mountain with about four hundred of his men. David wasn't just going to get his fair share of the food. The angry David was going to kill Nabal and every man that worked for him! "It isn't fair," David muttered as he marched. "I took care of this fellow's property, and he's paid me back evil for good. I'm going to get him!"[3]

Back at Nabal's house, some of the shepherds David had helped came to Nabal's wife, Abigail. They told Abigail how David had helped. Quickly Abigail gathered bread and meat and grain, and collected pressed cakes and raisins and figs. She loaded all the food on donkeys,

[1]Do you think it was fair for David's hungry men to be given some of Nabal's harvest? What would you do if someone had helped you, and when he was hungry asked only for some of your extra food?

[2]How do you think David will feel when he hears? What do you think David should do?

[3]Do you think David had good reason for being angry? What about David's plan to kill Nabal and his men? Why do you suppose people want to hurt others when they are angry? Have you ever felt about anyone like David felt about Nabal? (Share times when you have felt angry too.)

It was all right for David to feel angry. David hadn't been treated fairly. But what David planned wasn't right.

100

and she headed toward the mountain where David was. On the way she met the angry David, marching at the head of his men coming down to kill Nabal.

When Abigail saw David, she got off her donkey and bowed low. She apologized to David, and begged him to pay no attention to the wicked things Nabal had said. And then Abigail was very brave. She spoke up to David. She said, "It's not right to take revenge by hurting and killing your enemy. God has sent me to keep you from sinning. God punishes His people who sin."[4]

When David heard Abigail tell him he was planning to do wrong, David thanked her. "Praise the Lord for sending you to me today," David said. "May you be blessed for your good judgment, and for keeping me from bloodshed today. If you hadn't found me, I would have done wrong and killed Nabal."

So David took the food Abigail brought for his men, and went back to the mountain. The next morning Nabal heard what his wife had done. Nabal was so upset he had a heart attack, and died! God punished David's enemy. David didn't have to take revenge at all.[5]

> *Action Idea* With your children make up a list of things to do when you feel angry—and things not to do. The list might include:
> *Don't try to hurt the other person back.
> *Don't plan revenge.
> *Tell God how you feel about the unfair situation.
> *Tell your feelings to a parent or friend who can help you as Abigail helped David.
> *Be ready to accept an apology.
> *If the other person really sinned, let God pay them back instead of you. Remember, no one really gets away with sin.
> One important thing. You might plan how to help each other when you feel angry. Promise that if one of you feels angry, he or she will talk about it with one of the family. It's all right to express feelings verbally. And talking does help our feelings change. It is not all right to do wrong or to take revenge.

[4] *How do you think David liked to have Abigail tell him what he planned to do was a sin? What's the difference between feeling angry with someone and planning to do something to hurt them?*

[5] *What lesson do you think David learned? How would you explain that lesson to someone else? When do you think you need to remember the lesson yourself?*

David Spares King Saul
1 Samuel 24, 26

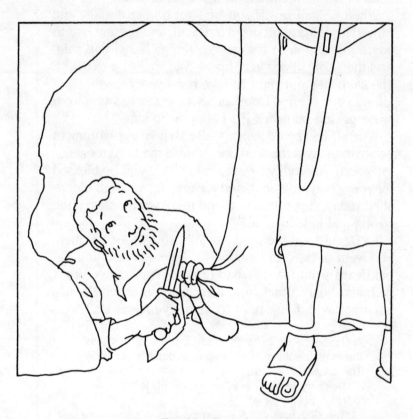

Would it be safer to kill Saul or cut off a piece of his robe?

Background It's hard enough to do the right thing. It's even harder when friends are urging us, telling us it's all right to do something that we are sure isn't right.

People of the Bible experienced the same kinds of pressures. At times the pressures to do wrong were even greater on them than on us and our children.

Jealous King Saul finally decided he must kill David. David had been a faithful officer in Saul's army, and a good friend to Saul's son, Jonathan. David was even married to Saul's daughter. But that didn't make any difference to Saul. Saul was so jealous of David that he was determined to kill him.

David ran and hid in the wilds of Israel, and was joined by friends who were loyal to him. But Saul called out his army and marched to find and kill this man he hated so much.

One time when Saul was chasing David with three thousand soldiers, David hid from Saul in the back of a deep cave. David and his men huddled in the darkness, waiting for Saul and his soldiers to go away. They must have been frightened back there. There was no other way out. If Saul discovered David's men, they would all be killed.

And then King Saul himself came into the cave!

"Quick!" one of David's friends whispered. "This is your chance! Kill King Saul and all your troubles will be over!"

All around David his friends whispered. "Kill Saul. Kill your enemy now!"[1]

David crept up in the darkness. He was so close he could reach out and touch King Saul! But Saul didn't even know David was there. In his mind David could hear all his friends, urging him to kill this king who was trying to kill him.

It didn't matter that his friends said it was all right. David knew he would have to decide for himself what was right.[2]

David reached out with his sharp knife. But he didn't plunge the knife into Saul. All David did was cut off a piece of Saul's clothing. Saul never even felt him do it.

Saul left the cave, called his soldiers, and marched on down into the valley.

When Saul was gone, David's friends were upset. "You could have killed him, David! Why didn't you listen to us!"

[1]How would you feel if all your friends urged you to do something, and said it was all right to do? Has that ever happened to you? Tell about that time and what happened.

[2]What do you suppose David will do? What would David do if he wanted to please his friends? What do you think God would want David to do? Why?

David told his friends they were wrong. "Saul was anointed king in God's name. Even if he is a bad king, and is trying to kill me, I don't have the right to fight back against him." David knew that God would protect David if he did what was right. So David was determined to please God first.

When Saul and his soldiers were down in the valley, David came out of the cave and called to Saul. David showed Saul the piece cut from his coat. He said to Saul, "Some of my friends urged me to kill you just now. But I spared you. Please, see that I am not guilty of rebellion or wrongdoing. I haven't harmed you, but you are trying to kill me."

David told Saul one more thing. "God will punish you for what you do wrong. But I will not touch you or harm you."[3]

[3]Do you think David felt good about what he had done, or bad? Why? How do you suppose your friends feel if you decide to do what you believe is right instead of what they want you to do?

Saul felt ashamed when David spoke to him. He stopped chasing David that time. But later the jealous Saul tried to kill David again and again. Finally Saul was killed in a battle with the Philistines.

> **Action Idea** Make a list of things friends sometimes urge your children to do which your boys and girls do not think are right, or are not sure about. Talk over those situations which recur most often. It may be helpful to your children to role play situations together, and practice different ways of saying no to peer pressure.
>
> Whenever one of your children does tell of successfully resisting peer pressure, express your own appreciation. Also express your assurance that God, who watched over and approved of David, is watching and is pleased with them.

David Confesses His Sin
2 Samuel 11, 12

How does it feel to be caught doing something wrong?

Background Conscience has two dimensions. In one, conscience moves us toward what is right. The other dimension condemns us for what we do wrong. But even the sense of guilt is a gift of God. Guilt is not intended to bind us, powerless, to our past. Guilt feelings are intended to point us to God, to seek forgiveness.

The story of David and Bathsheba is an adult story, in our modern X-rated sense. It is certainly not necessary to try to explain all the details to our children. But this incident did stimulate David to write one of the Bible's most powerful psalms—a psalm of deeply felt guilt, and great relief in forgiveness.

Davon was a good person, who trusted God. Usually David tried to please the Lord. But David was like everyone else. There were times when David did wrong.

One of those times happened after David became king. David was standing on the roof of his palace. Looking out at the rooftops below him, he saw a beautiful woman. David watched her, wishing that she was his wife.

She wasn't his wife, of course. She was married to one of David's army captains. But this time David didn't stop to think about pleasing God. David wanted her as a wife, anyway.[1]

David didn't stop at all. He just sent for the woman to come to his house, and be just like his wife.[2]

After David did this wrong thing, he didn't say anything to anyone. David even pretended that everything was all right. But deep inside David felt very guilty. Later David wrote poems that we have in the Bible book of Psalms. These psalms tell how he felt inside, even when he was trying to pretend to everyone else that everything was all right. One poem says:

When I kept silent,
    my bones wasted away
    through my groaning all day long.
For day and night
    your hand was heavy upon me;
my strength was sapped
        as in the heat of summer (Psalm 32:3, 4)

Inside David felt weak and miserable. He may have looked happy outside, but he was groaning deep inside.[3]

David didn't realize it, but those unhappy feelings were God's messengers. In fact, when we feel guilty today, those feelings are one way the Lord talks to us. The feelings tell us that we have done wrong and need to be forgiven.

But David didn't listen to those feelings inside. He tried to pretend to himself that he hadn't done wrong. So God sent a prophet named Nathan to David. Nathan

[1]*Have you ever wanted something, or wanted to do something, that you knew was wrong? (Share a time you felt a strong desire to do something you knew was wrong.)*

[2]*How do you think David felt after he did this? Do you think he was happy, or unhappy? How have you felt after you did something you knew was wrong?*

[3]*Do you suppose you've ever felt guilty? What had you done to make you feel that way?*

came to the palace of King David. Nathan came right up to the king's throne. And Nathan bravely told King David that David had sinned and deserved to be punished.

Finally David was ready to admit he had sinned. Humbly David prayed to God:

> Have mercy on me, O God,
>> according to your unfailing love;
>
> according to your great compassion . . .
>> cleanse me from my sin (Psalm 51:1, 2).[3]

When David asked for forgiveness, he didn't ask God to forgive because David deserved it. When we do something wrong, we deserve to be punished. But David asked God for mercy "according to your unfailing love," and "according to your great compassion." God forgives us because He loves us in spite of our sin.

Like David, you and I will do what pleases God most of the time. But sometimes we'll do something wrong. How good it is to know that we can come to God then and confess our sin, and God will forgive us.

Action Idea It will probably be helpful to your children if you memorize together the verses from Psalm 51 quoted in this story. Repeat them together several times in subsequent days and weeks. When you do, link the verses with guilt feelings. You want any violation of your children's conscience, and consequent guilt feelings, to trigger recall of this vital Bible passage, which turns thoughts to the lovingkindness of God, and to the forgiveness we receive from Him.

[3]*Do you think David deserved to be forgiven? What do you suppose God will do?*

David Sleeps
2 Samuel 15, 16; Psalm 3

Could you sleep if you knew enemy soldiers were looking for you?

Background Bedtime fears, and fear of the dark, are common for children six to eight. This particular Bible story tells of the time David was forced to leave Jerusalem because of the rebellion of his son, Absalom. Rushing out of the city, heartbroken at the faithlessness of his people as well as his son, David is traveling in the open when night falls. Pursued by enemies, almost alone, David peers into the gathering dark. Surely no one could have criticized David if his thoughts were filled with dark foreboding and fears.

108

"**D**avid!"

King David turned slowly and looked at the excited messenger.

"King David!" the man shouted, breathing hard as if he had been running. "You've got to run! Your son Absalom has led a rebellion! All your people are following him!"

David knew that Absalom wanted to be king. But a rebellion? Why, Absalom would have to kill David before Absalom could become king.

David didn't hesitate. "Hurry," David said. "We've got to flee. If we don't leave right away, Absalom will be here and kill us all."

Without even waiting to pack, David rushed out of his palace. But most of his officials and friends didn't want to go with David. Many deserted David, and followed Absalom.

Hurrying, David and his few friends left the palace. They rushed out of the city of Jerusalem. Maybe they could go south and find faithful people who still wanted David as king.

David traveled as fast as he could. The few people who were with David kept looking back. Was that Absalom's army back there? No, it was just the dust raised by a herd of cattle. But as they hurried most of them were afraid. Absalom's army might be right behind them! The army might catch up with them that night, when it was dark, and kill them all.

Soon it was too dark for David's party to travel any more. Even the moon didn't seem to want to come out. Only a few stars were there in the sky. Down below, David and his few friends sat in the dark, pulling blankets around their shoulders. As they sat there, they must have worried that their enemies were creeping up on them even then.[1]

David was very sad that night, as well as afraid. The people David had led as king didn't want him any more. They were even trying to kill him. David may have

[1]*What else do you suppose they might have been afraid of, there in the dark? (If you remember your childhood fears of the dark, tell something about them.) Do you ever feel scared in the dark? What do you worry about at night?*

looked around at the dark fearfully, too. But then David began to think about God.

All his life, God had been David's friend. David had tried to please the Lord, and David knew God had helped him. So David talked to God.

"You are a shield around me," David said (Psalm 3:3). Thinking about God, David began to lose his fear. Later David wrote another poem about that night.

"I lie down and sleep;
    I wake again, because the Lord sustains me.
I will not fear the tens of thousands
    drawn up against me on every side" (Psalm 3:5, 6).
Because God was a shield for David, protecting him from every danger, David could go to sleep, even there in the dark.

> ***Action Idea*** Let the clear message of the story sink into the awareness of your child. It's likely if your child is afraid of the dark he or she will want to hear this story often.
>
> You may also want to work together with your child to make a shield-shaped poster for his or her bedroom. "You are a shield around me, O Lord" or "I lie down and sleep . . . the Lord sustains me" are appropriate verses that might be printed on it.

Elijah Runs Away
1 Kings 19

What do you suppose Elijah is afraid of?

Background This story builds on a question: How should you and I react when our children are afraid? And on the corollary of that question: How does God react when His children fear?

This Bible story demonstrates God's wonderful gentleness with us. He is not angry when we're afraid. He does not shame or ridicule us. Instead, the Lord is very gentle, supporting us when we need support, and speaking in quiet, loving tones to reassure us that we are safe.

This Bible story will not only encourage your children. It is a story which provides an example for you and me of how good parents respond to children who are afraid.

"God," the prophet Elijah cried out, "show Your people who is really God, so they will trust You once again!"

Elijah was standing on Mount Carmel, with his arms lifted up in prayer. Thousands of the people of Israel were watching. In front of Elijah was a stone altar. The wood and a sacrifice on it were soaking with water.

For years an evil king and queen had led God's people to worship idols. Now Elijah was ready to prove to Israel that the Lord is the only true God.

"God," Elijah cried out. And as soon as Elijah prayed, fire came down from heaven. The fire from God burned up the water. It burned up the sacrifice and the wood. The fire even burned up the stones and the ground around the altar. God had performed a great miracle. When God's people saw it, they fell on the ground and cried out, "The Lord, He is God! The Lord really *is* God!"

How strong and powerful Elijah must have felt then. God had answered Elijah's prayer. God's people knew again that the Lord is the only true God.

But the evil king and queen weren't happy at all. They hated God. So the queen sent Elijah a message. "I am going to have you killed by this time tomorrow!"[1]

Elijah might have laughed at the queen. Elijah knew God was powerful. Elijah knew God answered his prayers. But for some reason that Elijah himself couldn't understand, all Elijah felt was fear! In fact, Elijah was so afraid that he just wanted to run away. He didn't think about God. He didn't think about anything. He just felt afraid—and he ran.[2]

Elijah ran and ran, because he was afraid. Elijah ran past the last town on the edge of a desert, and traveled out further into the desert. Finally Elijah was so exhausted he couldn't run any more. He just slumped down on the ground, all worn out, and wished he could die.

I'm no good at all, Elijah thought. Elijah was so ashamed of himself that he asked God to let him die.

[1]*What do you suppose Elijah will do now? Do you think you'd be afraid of a queen after God had just answered your prayer with a miracle?*

[2]*Sometimes everyone feels afraid, even when there isn't a good reason. When is the last time you felt afraid? How do you think other people would feel about you if they knew you were afraid?*

You might think that God would be angry with His prophet. Or that God would be ashamed of Elijah. But God sent an angel to bring Elijah food and water. God didn't say any angry word to Elijah. God comforted Elijah, and told him to rest.

Elijah did rest. After Elijah had slept a while, God's angel touched him gently. "You're all worn out," the angel said comfortingly. "Here, eat and drink some more."[3]

We all have times when we are afraid. Sometimes we even run away. God still loves us when we're afraid. God will always love us, and He will help us get over our fear.

[3]*How did God react when Elijah was afraid and ran away? How do you know from the story that God wasn't angry with Elijah?*

> ***Action Idea*** Work together on a "family agreement." You might want to agree together that when one of the children feels afraid of anything, he will come and tell a parent about it. Often talking about what we're afraid of can help. You will also want to agree that anyone who feels afraid will not be ridiculed or made fun of, and that parents won't be angry. Instead, like God, mom and dad will try to comfort and to help. You might add a third clause to the agreement. Together you and the child will tell God about the fear, and ask God to help your child even as He helped Elijah.

Naboth's Vineyard
1 Kings 21

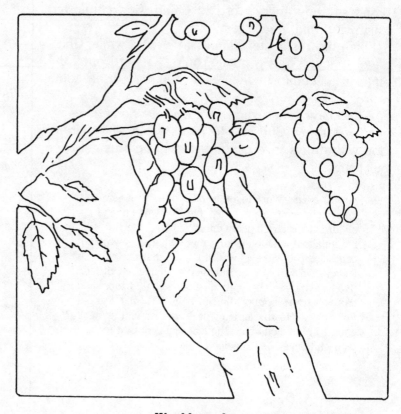

Would you hurt someone else just to get his field of grapes?

Background Children want things. This is understandable in children. They're so oriented to touch and feel and do. And, of course, TV constantly bombards them with the same message it carries to adults: have this toy, use this product, and you'll be happy. It's hard enough for adults to see through our attractive but superficial materialism. We shouldn't be surprised if our children are tempted to think that happiness for them is wrapped up in having something their friends have. We shouldn't be too surprised if, at some time or another, one of our children simply takes something he feels he must have.

114

Sitting in the palace, King Ahab could see the field of grapevines that belonged to Naboth.

"I want it," Ahab said to himself. "I like that field. It would make a good garden." So Ahab went to see Naboth.

"Let me have your vineyard," King Ahab said. "I'll trade you another vineyard for it, or give you money."

But Naboth was shocked. "Why, Your Majesty," Naboth said, "this field has been in my family since God gave us this land. I can't give you what I inherited from my fathers."

King Ahab was upset and angry. Ahab was king. He should be able to have whatever he wanted! At least, that's what Ahab thought. So Ahab sulked. He lay down on his bed, stuck out his lower lip, and wouldn't talk to anyone. Ahab wouldn't even eat. If he couldn't have that field where Naboth's grapevines grew, he just didn't want *anything*.[1]

Ahab's wife, Queen Jezebel, heard that her husband was sulking. She came in to see him. "Why are you so sullen?" Jezebel asked. "Why won't you eat?"

In a whining tone of voice Ahab told her. "Naboth won't give me his vineyard."[2]

Queen Jezebel didn't try to help Ahab see that he was being foolish. Jezebel didn't try to help Ahab be thankful for the things he did have. What Jezebel did was a terrible thing. "You're king," she told Ahab. "You can have what you want. Get up. I'll get that vineyard for you."

Queen Jezebel made up a plan to steal the vineyard. She knew that she couldn't steal it while Naboth was there to watch out for his property. So she plotted to accuse Naboth of a crime, and have him killed.

And she did just that!

Just because King Ahab wanted something he couldn't have, the evil queen plotted to steal it. And even to kill for it. Nothing is important enough to steal for. Nothing is important enough to hurt other people

[1] Have you ever known anyone who acted that way when he didn't get what he wanted? What words do you suppose tell how Ahab felt? Do you think King Ahab was right to feel sorry for himself, just because he couldn't have something he wanted?

[2] How about things you wanted, and did get? (Give an illustration ". . . like that truck you asked for at Christmas.") How long did it make you happy? Do you think you could be happy now if you didn't have it? What are some of the things people really need to make them happy and well? (Develop a list with your children.)

115

[3]Do you suppose it's wrong for us to want something we don't have? When do you think it becomes wrong? It may be foolish for us to think that some of the things we want will make us happy. But wanting things is only wrong when we do something wrong, like stealing, to get the things we want.

for. And later God punished both King Ahab and Queen Jezebel for the terrible things they did.[3]

Action Idea Exodus 22:7–9 sets out a simple principle for dealing with stealing. The thief is to pay back double for what he or she has taken. Restitution is not enough, for it only means return of what was taken. Restitution doubled provides a consequence which is likely to deter future thefts, and repay the person for any mental anguish during the period of loss.

It is always helpful to establish beforehand with children the consequences of wrong actions, and then to follow through faithfully in seeing that the consequences are paid. You may want to use this biblical principle in setting out ways you will deal with any future incidents of stealing.

God gave each family its own farm when the Israelites conquered the Promised Land. Boundary stones were set up to show what family owned each farm. Naboth would not give wicked King Abab the land God had given his family so long before.

Elisha Is Protected by Angels
2 Kings 6

How can we feel safe even when we seem to be in danger?

Background It's easy not to be afraid when mom and dad are near. Somehow, most children feel that their parents will be able to cope. All too often, children feel they are *not* able to cope in situations which hold some real or imagined terror.

Because fears are so common with young children, and with older boys and girls as well, several Bible stories deal with fear. Each story approaches fear from a slightly different perspective. Some try to help a child reevaluate what he fears. Others try to help him feel more able to cope. Some, like this Bible story, seek to help your child feel protected.

117

The king of Aram was angry. His army had been trying to trap the king of Israel. The king set up his
army camp in what he thought was the best place. But
every time the Israeli army avoided the trap.

"Who is the spy?" the king of Aram shouted one day.
"The king of Israel knows everything we plan."

His generals looked very serious. No one wanted to
be called a spy for the enemy. Then one of the officers
explained to the king.

"Your majesty, there is a prophet of God in Israel,
named Elisha. It's his fault. God tells the prophet what
we plan, and then Elisha warns the king of Israel."

The king of Aram rubbed his hands thoughtfully.
"Then, all we have to do is kill Elisha!"

So the king of Aram shouted out his order. "Go, find
out where Elisha is. Then send out some soldiers and
capture him."

When spies found out where Elisha was, a large army
of chariots and soldiers marched all night. They came
to the little town of Dothan, and they surrounded the
town. Now Elisha was trapped ! No one could get in the
city. And no one could get out.

When the sun started to come up, very early in the
morning, Elisha's servant went outside for some fresh
air. Suddenly he gasped, and ran inside. "Elisha!
Elisha!" he called. "There's an enemy army all around
the city! Oh, Elisha, what will we ever do!"[1]

Elisha's servant grabbed the prophet by his sleeve,
and pulled Elisha outside. Surely when Elisha saw the
enemy army out there Elisha would be afraid too.

But Elisha didn't seem afraid at all. Elisha looked at
the enemy soldiers. Elisha saw their chariots, and their
spears. Elisha saw they were all around the little town.

And then Elisha said something very strange to his
servant. "Don't be afraid. There are a lot more than they
have on our side."

The servant's mouth hung open. He looked all
around. There wasn't a single soldier of Israel anywhere
in sight. The servant and Elisha were all alone.

[1]*How do you think
Elisha's servant felt
when he saw the enemy
army? What do you
think he was afraid
might happen?*

Before the servant could say anything more, Elisha prayed. "God," he said, "please let my servant see what is really here." There, between Elisha and the enemy army, was a great army of angels. They were bright and shining and glowed like flames of fire. God was protecting His people. Even when Elisha and his servant seemed to be alone, God's angels were there to take care of them.[2]

The Bible says that angels serve and take care of God's children (cf. Heb. 1:14). So angels are here, to take care of you and me too. We may not be able to see angels. But we know God is caring for us, even when we feel afraid and alone.

> **Action Idea** Why not help your children make—or give each of them—small angel symbols to tape on school books or possessions. Or if you're good at sewing, sew angels on shirts and dresses and jeans where other children have foxes and alligators. Simple reminders that God's unseen angels are with our children can comfort them and help them cope.

[2]*How do you think the servant felt when he saw the angels? Have you ever felt afraid because it looked like you were alone? Can you tell me about that time? Would it have helped you if you knew angels were there, taking care of you, too? How would it have helped?*

Hezekiah Is Healed
2 Kings 20

Would you jump for joy if God answered your prayer for healing?

Background Sickness is common in childhood. Measles and colds and tummy aches all come, and afterward are soon forgotten. Boys and girls live much in the here and now. They don't think back about sicknesses, or ahead. But some sicknesses are serious. It's then that children are likely to be concerned. This is especially true if they sense the anxiety of older members of the family.

There are many things that parents can do to reduce the fears of boys and girls, and to deal wisely with serious illness. In addition, there is the path taken by godly King Hezekiah when he was terminally ill. We can turn to God in prayer. God will not always answer our prayer for healing as we wish. But we and our children can be sure that God does hear. And that God cares.

King Hezekiah was a good man. He loved God, and all the years Hezekiah was king over God's people, he tried to rule them wisely. Hezekiah also encouraged his people to worship God. Hezekiah was one of the best kings God's Old Testament people ever had.

You'd think maybe that such a good king would live for a long, long time. But one day when Hezekiah wasn't old at all he became very sick. The days passed, and Hezekiah didn't get better. Hezekiah grew worse. Finally Hezekiah was so sick that everyone was sure he was about to die.

God hadn't forgotten Hezekiah though. God didn't want this good king to think the Lord had forgotten him. So God sent the prophet Isaiah to speak to Hezekiah.

Isaiah didn't have good news. "Hezekiah," Isaiah said, "God has told me that you will not recover from this sickness." God knew what was happening. God wanted Hezekiah to know that the Lord cared, even if Hezekiah wasn't going to get well.[1]

Hezekiah must have been glad to know God still loved him. Sometimes sick people forget that God loves them and feel that they are being punished. But what Hezekiah now wanted most of all was to get well. Hezekiah knew that someday he would die. But he didn't want to die now.

So Hezekiah prayed. "O Lord," Hezekiah prayed, "remember how I have tried as hard as I could to do what pleases You." Hezekiah cried too, asking the Lord to please make him well.[2]

Hezekiah prayed very hard that God would make him well. God heard that prayer, and God had a very special answer. Before Isaiah the prophet got outside the king's palace, God spoke to Isaiah. "Go back to Hezekiah," the Lord told Isaiah. "Tell Hezekiah that the Lord has heard your prayer, and said 'Yes. I will let you live for fifteen more years. You will not die from this sickness.'"

Then Isaiah told the doctors the medicine to use for Hezekiah. And King Hezekiah began to get well.

[1] *Even people God loves don't always get well when they are sick. Do you think Hezekiah was glad to know that God still loved him anyway? What do you suppose Hezekiah wanted most?*

[2] *Do you think God will answer Hezekiah's prayer? God hears all our prayers, and He answers them all. But sometimes God says "No" to what we ask. Do you suppose God doesn't love us when He says "No"?*

God had heard the prayer of good King Hezekiah when he was sick. God had said, "Yes" when Hezekiah prayed that he might get well.[3]

[3]How do you know what to pray for (the sick person)? What shall we say to God? Let's pray for him (her) now.

Action Idea One of the most meaningful things we can do to build our own children's confidence in prayer is to make a "we asked"—"God answered" record book. The book should not only contain a list of requests for friends or family who are sick. It can contain a list of all the daily concerns of adults and children that are brought to the Lord.

Cultivating the practice of prayer is something we adults need to do as well. Making an answer book to keep a record of family prayers will be as enriching to us as it is to our boys and girls.

Esther Does What Is Right
Esther

Can't a woman be beautiful and brave too?

Background The Book of Esther tells the true story of a young Jewish woman, chosen to be queen of a vast pagan empire nearly 500 years before Christ. When Esther's people are threatened in an empire-wide plot, the young queen must decide whether to risk her life and try to help, or to keep silent and perhaps be safe.

The Book of Esther is another of the great books of our Old Testament which reads like a story. Your family will enjoy reading the whole tale as a continued story, one which can extend for nine exciting mealtime or bedtime adventures.

This retelling focuses on the choice which Esther had to make. Like Esther we and our children often find ourselves facing similar decisions. Will we speak up for what is right, or keep silent? Will we be God's agents for good, or hold back?

123

Haman smiled cruelly as he left the king of the great Persian Empire. Haman had the king's permission! Now he would have revenge on his enemy!

Of course, Mordecai [Mor-dek-i] the Jew wasn't much of an enemy. Mordecai was just a minor official at the palace, a clerk in one of the courtyards of the palace. But whenever Haman walked through the palace, everyone else bowed down. That is, everyone kneeled down but Mordecai. Mordecai didn't seem to know how important Haman, the king's favorite friend, was!

And that made Haman angry.

Haman was very, very proud. And Haman decided to get revenge on Mordecai.

But the cruel Haman was so proud that it wasn't enough for him to hurt just Mordecai. Haman decided that he would have all of Mordecai's people killed too. Mordecai was a Jew.

That's why Haman was smiling as he left the king. He'd asked the king for a favor.

Haman had told the king of Persia there was a troublesome race of people in the empire. It would be better, Haman told the king, if those nasty Jews were all killed.

The king had nodded.

"Do what you please with them."

So Haman left the king with permission to kill all the Jews in the world.

Haman hurried and wrote orders to be sent throughout the empire. On a certain day, people were allowed to kill Jews and to take their property. On that day, Haman thought gleefully, the people of his enemy Mordecai, who wouldn't kneel when Haman came by, would all die.

Mordecai did not kneel down before Haman because Mordecai worshiped God, not powerful men in the Persian Empire. When Mordecai heard of the decree that Haman had sent throughout the world, he knew that somehow God would protect His own people, the Jews. But how? Once an order was sent out in the king of

Persia's name, no one could change it, not even the king. That was the law in Persia. Even the king couldn't change his own orders.

But there was one thing that the king of Persia didn't know. There was one thing that the wicked Haman didn't know. That thing was that the new young queen of Persia, Esther, was a Jew too! Esther was a cousin of Mordecai. Mordecai had brought her up as if she were his own daughter. So Mordecai went to see Esther.

Mordecai sent Esther a copy of the king's order, and begged Esther to go to the king and beg for mercy for her people.

Esther was afraid.

"Don't you know," she sent a message back to Mordecai, "if anyone goes to see the king without being sent for, that person will be put to death? Only if the king raises his golden scepter will the guards spare that person's life."[1]

Sometimes it's very hard for us to speak up when others are doing something wrong. Esther thought she might be safe if she kept quiet. So Esther sent a message back to Mordecai and told him she was afraid.[2]

Mordecai sent a message back to Esther. He told her, "If you don't speak up, God will find another way to save our people. But have you thought? Maybe you have become queen just so you will be able to speak up at this time!"

Esther was still afraid.

But the more she thought, the more she realized Mordecai was right. She was Queen. She could try to go to the king. So Esther should be the one to ask for the life of her people.

Esther sent another message to Mordecai. "Please, ask everyone not to eat, but to pray for the next three days. After three days, I will go and speak to the king, even though it is against Persian law. And if I am killed, well, I will be killed."[3]

Three days later, Esther did go to the king. The king didn't have her killed. In fact, because Esther was brave

[1] How do you suppose Esther felt about speaking up? What do you think she thought about? Do you ever have times when you see others doing something wrong, and wonder if you ought to speak up? Can you tell about a time when that's happened to you? How did you feel?

[2] What would you tell Esther if you were there? What would you tell friends who are afraid to speak up when they see other people doing things that are wrong?

[3] Do you suppose Esther felt better when she decided to do the right thing and speak up? Was she still afraid? What helps you decide to do the right thing, even when you are afraid?

125

and did the right thing even when she was afraid, the Jewish people were saved.

God used Esther and Mordecai and other things that happened to ruin Haman's evil plan. In the end the king of Persia had Haman hung, and God's people were saved!

If you'd like to find out how, we can read the whole story at mealtimes (bedtimes) from the Bible.

Action Idea Read the whole book, and keep a record of the circumstances which play such a key part in this true Bible story. After reading each chapter, talk about how God seems to have arranged the circumstances to save His people. Talk too about the fact that God doesn't need to use miracles to help us today. God takes care of us without our even knowing it. Because God is in control, we can be like Esther. We can choose to do the right thing even when it seems dangerous or hard to do.

Daniel in the King's School
Daniel 1

How do friends help us choose what is right?

Background Daniel was probably in his early teens when he was brought with a group of Judean captives to Babylon. It was the policy of King Nebuchadnezzar to train promising upper-class youths from subject nations as administrators for his kingdom. Daniel and three other Jewish youths were placed in this "king's school." The four were given Babylonian names, clothing, and food. If they passed their examinations, their destiny was to live in the capital of that alien land.

One of the significant facts of life for our boys and girls is that they are influenced by each other and not just by adults. Daniel's firm decision to follow the Lord helped his friends stand firm. Daniel's respectful attitude toward those who unwittingly wanted him to do wrong won the day. Our boys and girls can learn much about how to take a stand for what is right, and how to be sensitive to others, from this familiar Bible story.

127

"**A**ll right," said Ashpenaz, looking over the teen-aged boys lined up in front of him. "We'll take him . . . and him . . . and him. And oh yes, be sure to take that one. The one they call Daniel."

For two days Ashpenaz, an official of the Babylonians who had taken thousands of God's people captive, questioned and tested the sons of the Israelite nobility. Ashpenaz was looking for the smartest boys, who were also handsome and athletic. King Nebuchadnezzar had given him strict orders. "Take the best of them," the king said. "Teach them the Babylonian language, and teach them our ways." The teens selected were to be trained in the king's school for three years, and then would serve the king as officials in Babylon.

The soldiers motioned the four boys whom Ashpenaz chose. "You four!" one said harshly. "Come this way."

So Daniel, Shadrach, Meshach and Abednego marched away from their friends, and were taken to the king's school.

At the school the boys were treated well. They were given a place to sleep and to study. The boys were even given the kind of food and wine that the king himself ate and drank.

But that was the problem! In the Bible God told the Jewish people they were to eat only certain kinds of food. The people of Babylon didn't follow God's rules for the Jews. So the food that was brought to Daniel and his friends was food Jewish people were not allowed to eat!

Daniel made up his mind.

Daniel determined he would obey God and not eat the Babylonian food. Daniel boldly told his three friends what he planned.[1]

It was hard for Daniel and his three friends, in the king's school, to decide to keep God's rules for the Jews. But when Daniel took the lead, his friends followed.[2]

Daniel knew that he would have to obey God. But he also knew he should be polite to the Babylonian offi-

[1] *Sometimes we help other people choose what's right by speaking up for it. Can you think of a time some friend helped you do what you knew was right, by saying he or she would do it? Have you ever been the leader for your friends, spoken up for doing right?*

[2] *Who is the friend who most helps you do what is right? Do you like being with this friend? Why, or why not?*

cials. So very politely Daniel asked the officer in charge for permission not to eat the king's food. The officer shook his head when Daniel asked him for a special diet.

"The king himself ordered your food and drink. What if I let you eat your special diet, and you don't look as healthy as the other young men in the school? Why, the king would have me killed for something like that!"

Daniel understood why the officer was afraid. He wasn't upset or angry. He could see the officer was worried and not just being mean.

So very politely Daniel said to the officer, "Please let us try our diet for ten days. Just give us vegetables and water, and see how we look after that."

The officer agreed to this test. And at the end of the ten days, Daniel and his friends looked healthier and stronger than those who ate the royal food. So the officer took away the rich food and drink of the king, and let Daniel and his friends eat only food allowed the Jews in God's law.

God does help us do right. And it's good to have friends who also want to obey God, who will do what is right too.

> ***Action Idea***   Make a list of friends. Talk about three
> different traits. Which are friends who will choose what
> is right and do it—if someone else does right first?
> Which are friends who will take the lead and do what is
> right, no matter what others do? Which are friends who
> will do right or wrong, depending on what other chil-
> dren they are with do? The kinds of friends we want to
> have as "best friends" are boys and girls whom we can
> help to please God, and who will help *us* to please Him.

Daniel in the Lions' Den
Daniel 6

When is it hard to remember we are surrounded by God's love?

Background Why are fears of wild animals so prominent among young children? It's hard to tell. Perhaps to children they represent everything that is strange and different and, thus, beyond their control. Whatever the reason, such fears are extremely common. Wild animals are real, even though they may not be near.

But while situations may be out of your control or out of mine, they are never out of God's control. This is the comforting message communicated so powerfully in the familiar story of Daniel in the lions' den.

Slowly Daniel kneeled down beside his open window. He turned to face the far-off city of Jerusalem, where the temple of God once stood, and he began to pray.

"See!" came an excited whisper.

Several men were hiding in bushes outside Daniel's window. Now they pointed at the praying Daniel and smiled wickedly at each other. "I told you so," said the leader of Daniel's enemies. "I told you he'd never stop praying to his God. We've got old Daniel at last!"

Then the men hurried away to tell the king about Daniel.

You see, Daniel was a high official in the Persian kingdom. Daniel was in charge of other officials. And Daniel was very honest. So as long as Daniel was in charge, watching them, the other officials couldn't do anything dishonest.

Finally the Persian officials decided that they would have to get rid of Daniel. The officials watched Daniel carefully, looking for something to accuse Daniel of. But Daniel was trustworthy and hard-working. His enemies could never find anything bad to accuse Daniel about.

Then one of them had an idea. Everyone knew that Daniel loved the Lord and prayed to God at least three times a day. Maybe the evil officials could find some way to use that against Daniel. So the evil officials went to King Darius.

"You're such a great king, O Darius," they said, flattering him. "All your royal advisors and governors have agreed there's only one way to let everyone know how wonderful you are. You should write an order that, for thirty days, no one can ask anyone except you for anything. And, O yes. You're so great that no one should even pray to any god for thirty days."

Darius was flattered.

Yes, Darius thought, *I am great.* Without even wondering why Daniel wasn't there with the other officials, Darius wrote out the order.

The very first day the order was given, Daniel got up

and left his office at noon, as he always did. Daniel walked to his home. Daniel went up to his room and opened the window, as he always did. And Daniel prayed to the Lord.

Outside, Daniel's enemies watched and pointed and laughed. At last they had trapped Daniel! Daniel had disobeyed King Darius' order. And the penalty for disobeying the King? To be thrown into a den full of hungry lions![1]

While Daniel prayed, his enemies rushed to see King Darius. "King Darius!" their leader said. "You made a decree that anyone praying to any man or god but you would be thrown to the lions. We all saw Daniel, and he still prays three times a day to his God."

Then King Darius was very upset, because he liked Daniel. There was a law in Persia. No decree published by the king could be changed. Even Darius himself couldn't change what he had written. Darius tried. But King Darius couldn't figure out any way at all to rescue Daniel. Darius sadly gave the command to throw him to the lions. "I hope," Darius said to Daniel as the soldiers took him out, "I hope your God, whom you worship so faithfully, will rescue you."

The soldiers pushed Daniel inside the den full of fierce lions. The king himself sealed the door. Then Darius went back to his palace. But Darius couldn't sleep or even eat. All Darius did was walk back and forth, waiting to see what would happen to Daniel.

When dawn came, and the first light showed in the east, Darius hurried to the den of hungry lions. "Daniel," Darius called. "Daniel, servant of the living God. Has your God whom you worship so faithfully been able to rescue you from the lions?"

And Darius heard Daniel answer! "O King," Daniel's voice came from inside the lions' den. "God sent His angel, and the angel shut the mouths of the lions. The lions have not hurt me, because I've done nothing wrong."

And then King Darius remembered the men who had

[1]Why do you suppose Daniel disobeyed the king and prayed anyway? Do you suppose Daniel felt afraid when he prayed? Who do you think Daniel thought was more powerful, King Darius, or the Lord?

tricked him and tried to get Daniel killed. "Bring them here," the angry king said. And when the frightened enemies of Daniel were dragged in, Darius said, "Throw *them* to the lions!"

Those men didn't have an angel to protect them.

Those men didn't even believe in God.

And the lions leaped on them, and killed them immediately.

Later, Darius sent a letter through the Persian kingdom. "No one must ever say anything bad about Daniel's God, because He is the real and living God. Daniel's God is able to rescue the people who trust Him, and save them. He is a wonderful God, who rescued Daniel from the lions."[2]

> **Action Idea** To visualize the teaching of this story make a "circle of God's love" tableau. From construction paper, cut a large circle. Then draw or purchase a figure of a man. Stand the man inside the circle. Outside, place several lion figures, obtained from a hobby shop or drawn and cut out. Also cut out a picture of your child, and place it inside the circle with Daniel.
>
> Place the tableau as a centerpiece on your table, or in your child's room. Remind your child that God who protected Daniel from the lions protects us as well. We are safe inside the circle of God's love.

[2]*When are you most happy that God takes care of you? When is it hardest to remember God is with you to protect you?*

Jonah Is Helped to Do Right

Jonah

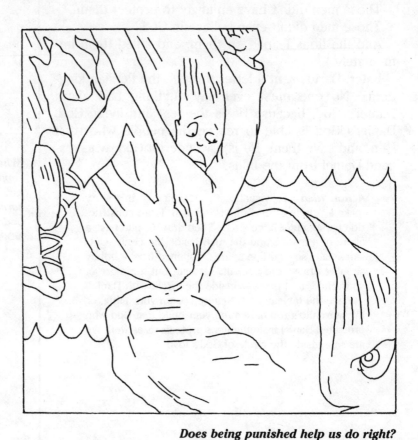

Does being punished help us do right?

Background Why do we discipline our children? Our goal is not really to punish. Our goal is to help our children learn to make right choices. Good discipline is corrective—not punitive.

Few stories in the Bible illustrate this so clearly as the story of the reluctant prophet, Jonah. Commanded to go north to Nineveh, Jonah disobeyed God and headed south! But God worked on in Jonah's life. God brought Jonah to the place where he would choose obedience.

134

"How much money will it cost me to travel with you to Tarshish?" the little man asked the sea captain. The captain thought a minute and named a price. The little man looked around, as if he were afraid someone was watching. Then he took out his purse, paid the captain, and hurried on board the sailing ship.

Mmmmm, thought the captain. *That man acts like he's running away.* But the captain didn't think about the little man for long. The captain had cargo to load. His ship was getting ready to sail.

Inside the ship, the little man, whose name was Jonah, found a quiet corner and went to sleep. He was so tired. Jonah had hurried all the way from his home city, rushing to the sea. Jonah was one of God's prophets. And God had sent Jonah on a mission.

There was only one thing.

God said, "Go north to Nineveh."

Jonah was going south. Jonah was disobeying God![1]

Jonah was so tired that he didn't even wake up when the ship put out to sea. Jonah didn't wake up when the wind filled the sails, and the ship moved out over the waves. In fact, Jonah didn't even wake up when it began to storm. The wind blew harder and harder. The waves got higher and higher. Everyone else on the ship was awake, all right. They were all terrified! The crew even threw the cargo overboard to make the ship lighter.

It was then they found Jonah, still asleep.

The captain woke up Jonah.

"How can you sleep like that?" the captain shouted. "Get up and pray! Maybe your God will notice us and we won't all drown."

As fhe storm grew worse, the men drew lots to find out if someone had done something wrong and if that was why the storm came.

Jonah drew the short straw! "Tell us," all the sailors said. "Who are you? Where are you from?"

Then Jonah confessed. "I am a Hebrew (Jew) and I worship the living God, who created the sea and the land."

[1] *How do you suppose God felt about Jonah disobeying Him? How do you suppose Jonah felt? What do you think God should do to Jonah? What happens to you when you disobey on purpose? Why do you suppose mom or dad do that to you?*

[2]Do you think God is
trying to kill Jonah?
Does God hurt or kill us
when we disobey Him?
God loves us too much
to want to hurt us. God
wants what is best for
us.

[3]Do you think God will
listen to Jonah's
prayers? Does God
listen to our prayers
when we have done
wrong? What do you
think Jonah will say to
God?

"Men," Jonah said, "this storm has come because of me. The only thing you can do is throw me overboard. then the ship will be safe.[2]

The sailors didn't want to throw Jonah overboard. They tried to row to shore. But the waves were too big. Finally the sailors asked God to forgive them and did what Jonah said. They picked Jonah up and threw him into the stormy sea. As soon as they did, the waters began to get calm again. The sailors knew now that God had sent the storm, and that God had made the storm stop.

When Jonah hit the water and began to sink, Jonah was sure he would drown. But before Jonah could drown, a great fish, specially prepared by God and sent to just that spot in the ocean, swallowed Jonah whole. Inside the great fish, Jonah finally began to pray![3]

The first thing Jonah prayed was "Help!"

And then Jonah prayed something else. Jonah promised God that he would go back home and do what God told him to do. You and I can always ask God for help. We can tell God we will obey the Lord again, even after we've done wrong.

Three days later the great fish threw Jonah up on a beach back in Israel. Then God told Jonah again. "Go north, to the city of Nineveh, and take them My message."

So Jonah went north.

God gave Jonah another chance to obey Him. Jonah was ready at last to do what God said.

Action Idea Talk about your family discipline practices. Explain that, like God, you discipline because you want your children to do the right thing. You do not want just to punish them. You want to help them do what is right.

Talk about incidents of discipline in the past few weeks or months. Have your punishments helped your children choose what is right? Would other discipline practices be of more help?

God Promises to Send His Son

Isaiah 7

When did God make the promise that Jesus would be born?

Background Prophecy is one great biblical theme which demonstrates God's truthfulness. God announces beforehand what will happen. God makes promises and keeps them. God's people can rely on what the Lord says will happen. Old Testament prophecy touches on many topics. One of the most common is that of the coming of a promised Savior. God has kept these Old Testament promises about Jesus. Because God has always kept His word, we can trust Him to keep His word in all things.

As parents we need to be truthful with our children. We need to help them see the importance of truthfulness in every interpersonal relationship. This Bible story will help your boys and girls think about the importance of being trustworthy, and help them explore their relationships with others.

King Ahaz was afraid.

Two nearby countries had agreed to attack Israel.

Ahaz's heart pounded. What could he do? The two countries were much stronger than his own land!

That's when God sent the prophet Isaiah to Ahaz with a promise. Isaiah, carrying his baby in his arms, met Ahaz and delivered God's message. "Don't worry," God told Ahaz. "They will not invade your country."

King Ahaz didn't feel happy about that promise. The king didn't feel relieved. Ahaz didn't even feel thankful. You see, Ahaz didn't really believe what God said.

God spoke again to Ahaz then. Isaiah the prophet told the king, "Ask God for some miracle as proof."

But Ahaz only shook his head. Ahaz wouldn't do what God said. "I will not ask," Ahaz said.[1]

God was upset with Ahaz. God always tells the truth. There was no reason Ahaz shouldn't believe what God said. Just to prove to everyone, everywhere, that we can always trust God, God made a special promise.

"One day," God had the prophet Isaiah say, "a young woman will have a child all by herself, without a man as the father. That special child will be a boy, and He will be God, come to be with us."

What a wonderful promise. God promised that His Son would come to earth and be born as a baby! What an impossible thing, some people might think. But it did happen, just as God promised. And you know who that special child was. Yes, it was Jesus. Seven hundred years before Jesus was born, God told us He was coming. And it happened, just as God said.[2]

Action Idea Together look up other promises in the Old Testament about Jesus' coming. See how each one was fulfilled. You can do this as a pre-Christmas activ-

[1] *How do you suppose God felt when Ahaz wouldn't believe God was telling the truth? Do you think God was telling the truth? Why? We can always trust God, because He always tells us the truth.*

[2] *God wants us to know we can always trust Him. So God always tells us the truth in the Bible.*

Most important, God wants us to learn to be like Him. Because God is the kind of Person everyone can trust, God wants you and me to be trustworthy persons too.

Let's thank God now that we can always trust Him, because He never lies to us or breaks His promises.

ity, as well as an activity linked with encouraging truth-fulness.

Important Old Testament promise passages are found in: Isaiah 9:1–2, 6, 7, 11:1, 53:9, 12; Micah 5:2; Zechariah 9:9, 11:12, 13; Psalm 22:18, 69:21, 22:1, 31:5, 34:20.

TALKABLE STORIES FROM THE GOSPELS

An Angel Visits Mary
Matthew 1; Luke 1

What made Mary praise God?

Background   Christmas is one of the two focal events of the Christian year. During this season we remember the Incarnation: the birth of Jesus as truly Man and fully God, to become our Savior. The meaning of Christmas can be clouded by the excitement of giving and receiving gifts. Its meaning can be distorted, as Santa replaces the Christ Child as central figure in winter's culminating drama. It is important that in our homes a special place for Jesus be retained.

Mary was sewing.

My goodness, she thought. *I'll never get this dress done in time. Now, where did I put that white thread?*

It was exciting to be sewing on these particular clothes. You see, Mary was engaged to be married. She was preparing the clothes she would bring to her new home when the marriage took place. Why, she and Joseph would be married in just ten more months. There was so much more to do!

We don't know just what Mary was doing one special night. But we do know something wonderful that happened to her. As Mary was working around her home, an angel came to her.

"Greetings, Mary," the angel said. "You are highly favored by God. The Lord is with you."

Mary was upset at first. After all, angels don't come and speak to people very often! Besides, Mary didn't know what the angel's words of greeting might mean.

The angel explained. "Don't be afraid, Mary. God plans something wonderful for you. You are going to have a baby boy, and you are to name Him Jesus. This child will be very great. He will be the Son of God, and will be King over an endless kingdom."

Mary was shocked. "But," she said to the angel, "how can I have a baby? I'm not even married!"

The angel answered Mary's question. "Your baby, Jesus, won't have a human father. God Himself will make the baby grow, so the holy child that you have will be the Son of God."

Mary didn't even wait to think about it. "I am the Lord's servant," she said. "Whatever God wants, I want it to happen too."

Then the angel left Mary to think about the wonderful and amazing promise God had made. Every other baby born into our world would have a human father and a human mother. But this baby, Jesus, would only have a human mother. God would be the Father of Jesus. Jesus would be the Son of God.

Later Mary made up a song to celebrate. She was so

happy about Jesus being born, that she wanted to sing for joy. Here is part of her song:

I praise the Lord,
   I am full of joy in God my savior.
God has remembered even me,
   and everyone will think of me as
   blessed to be Jesus' mother.
The Mighty God has done such great things for me—
He is holy,
   He is full of mercy for everyone
    who worships Him.

Mary must have sung her song of joy many times as Jesus' birth drew near. Now we all celebrate the birth of Jesus together. Sending Jesus to be our Savior is one of the most wonderful things God has ever done.

Action Idea Use the story to launch preparations for your own family celebration of this season. Let your children take part in all your preparations. One fun family project is to make up your own joy songs of celebration like Mary's. Pick a theme for your songs, such as "Jesus loves me" or "How Jesus helps me." When everyone has written their own poem (joy song), read them to each other. You may want to print them on large sheets of construction paper with a felt-tipped pen, and attach them to your walls. It's also traditional to decorate the house during the Christmas season. In keeping with the celebration theme, plan with your boys and girls how to make your home look joyful. Plan for the inside and, if you wish, the outside also. You'll also find it's fun for your children to visit a Christian bookstore and pick out tapes or records that can fill your home with joyful Christmas music.

Jesus Is Born
Matthew 1; Luke 2

Was a manger a good place to be born?

Background This is the second in a sequence of three stories which focus on Christmas. This season we remember the incarnation of Jesus: the great miracle which God performed when the eternal Son of God became a human being. The meaning of the Christmas season is not summed up in gifts or vacation or TV advertisements for expensive toys. The central figure at Christmas is not Santa, but Christ. Yet our goal at Christmas time is not to completely shut out the secular world, for this would be impossible. Our goal is simply, through family times together, and by the atmosphere of our home, to affirm the fact that Jesus is the One in whom we rejoice at this special time of year.

Mary swayed back and forth on the back of the little donkey.

Mary was tired. And the baby inside her seemed heavier than ever.

"How much further?" Mary asked Joseph.

"Not far now," Joseph said, as he walked along beside Mary and the donkey. "We're almost to Bethlehem."

How Joseph must have worried as the two of them came near the little town. Where would Mary stay? Bethlehem was a small town. There weren't hotels and motels. There was just a small inn where travelers could stay. But now many, many people would be coming back to Bethlehem to be counted. The inn might be full.

It was nearly night when Mary and Joseph came to Bethlehem. Mary's back ached from the baby and the long ride. Joseph was tired and dusty. Both of them were cold, because a chill wind blew. And just as Joseph had feared, the inn was full!

"But what can we do?" Joseph asked the innkeeper. "Where can we stay?"

The innkeeper shrugged. "I'm sorry," he said. "The town is just full. And my inn is full, too."

"It wouldn't be so bad," Joseph explained, "but my wife is just about have her baby."

The innkeeper looked at Mary. Yes, there was no doubt. She was going to have a baby. And soon!

"I'll tell you what," the innkeeper said. "I could let you stay in my stable. It's nice and warm, and there is soft straw to rest on. It's probably the best place you'll find here these days."

As soon as Mary went into the stable, she felt better. Friendly cows looked at her with warm, brown eyes. Young sheep moved close, to nuzzle her ankles curiously. Their bodies had warmed the air in the stable, and for the first time that day Mary began to feel warm herself. Gratefully she lay down to rest on a pile of straw. The straw felt so much softer than the back of that donkey! Before Mary knew it she had fallen asleep.

Later that evening Mary suddenly woke up. She could

feel the baby moving inside. She could feel her own body squeeze together, pushing the baby down further and further in her body. "Joseph," Mary whispered, "the baby! The baby is going to be born tonight."

That same night shepherds, living in nearby fields so they could take care of their flocks of sheep, saw something wonderful. An angel suddenly appeared, and they were surrounded by a bright, glowing light. The men were terrified. But the angel spoke to them. "Don't be afraid," the angel said. "I have good news . . . news of great joy for you and for everyone elsewhere. Today, in David's town of Bethlehem, the Savior has been born. He is the Christ, the Lord. And you will find the child lying in a manger, wrapped in strips of cloth."

Then many angels appeared. They sang and praised God.

When the angels left and returned to heaven, the shepherds talked excitedly to each other. "Let's go!" they said. "Yes. Let's go to Bethlehem. We want to see this wonderful thing the Lord has told us about."

The shepherds hurried toward Bethlehem, Mary, and her baby. Just as God had told Mary, the baby was a boy. Just as God had told her to, Mary named the baby Jesus. Looking down at her very first child, the very special child who would grow up to be our Savior, Mary was very happy.

Then the shepherds came. The shepherds pounded on the door of the inn. They told the innkeeper and all the guests about the wonderful things they had seen in the field. The shepherds told of the angels' songs of celebration, and the message from God that the promised Savior was born that night. And then everyone hurried to the stable, to see the baby.

The manger didn't seem a special place. But as everyone peered at Mary and her baby, and as the quiet animals watched, they all knew that this was the most special place of all. And this was the most special night of all. Jesus was born! God had kept His promises. The Son of God was here to be our Savior.

Action Idea Reconstruct the manger scene in your home. Plaster of Paris sets for molding Mary, Joseph, the baby, shepherds, and several animals are available during the Christmas season at hobby shops. Make casting and painting these figures—and setting up your own manger scene—a family project.

Babies born in Jesus' time didn't have diapers and little dresses. Babies were wrapped in strips of cloth called *swaddling clothes*. Mothers loved their babies then, just as mothers do now, and took good care of them.

The Wise Men Visit
Matthew 2

How far would you go to worship King Jesus?

Background   This is the third in a sequence of three stories for the Christmas season. With their *Action Ideas* these stories are designed to help you keep your family's focus on celebration of Jesus' birth.

This particular Christmas story can stimulate the practice followed in our home all during the children's growing-up years, of having a special family "birthday gift" for Jesus. Christmas day was not only a day we showed love to each other by giving gifts. It was a day during which we remembered God's gift of His Son, during which we gave to God our own special "thank you" gift.

150

Far away from Bethlehem where Jesus was born, wise men called Magi studied. They studied ancient books. They studied mathematics. They studied the stars. For hundreds of years Magi studied and learned many things. Each generation wrote down what it learned—and taught others. Studying wasn't very exciting. But learning was important. And so the Magi spent all their time trying to learn more.

Then one night something very exciting happened.

A special, bright star began to shine.

The Magi were very excited. What could that star mean? They studied all their old books. They studied the books of foreign countries, like the Old Testament books of the Jews. And finally they found out what that special, bright star meant!

"I've found it," one of them told the others. "The promised King of the Jews has been born. That's what the star means! God's Son has come to earth at last! Let's go see Him!"

The Magi had servants pack up special tents, for they would camp out while on the journey. They carefully selected the foods they would take along. They didn't want to be hungry on the journey. The wise men took soft bedding too. It wouldn't do to sleep on the ground.

"Now wait," one of the wise men said. "We have everything we need to live comfortably on our journey. God has taken good care of us. But God has done even more. God has given us His Son, as the star told us. What are we going to bring on our journey as a gift for the Baby King, to say 'thank you' to God?"

After thinking very hard, and planning very carefully, each wise man picked out his own special gift to give to Jesus. The gifts were packed, and the wise men started on their long journey.

Months later, the Magi came to Jerusalem. There they began to ask, "Where is the One who is born to be King of the Jews?"

When King Herod heard about the wise men and their question, he was upset. *He* was king, and Herod didn't want any other king around. So Herod called all the teachers of the Bible together and asked them an important question. "Where does the Bible say the Christ, the Son of God, will be born?" The wise men opened their Bibles. They knew the answer to that question! "King Herod, the prophet Micah has written that the great ruler of God's people will be born in Bethlehem" (cf. Micah 5:2).

So King Herod called the Magi to a secret conference. Herod asked them when the star first appeared. "Almost two years ago," the Magi told Herod. Then the king sent them to Bethlehem, to look for the child. "If you find the child," Herod said, "come back and report to me."

The happy Magi hurried off toward Bethlehem, just a few miles away. They had traveled so far, for so many months. As the Magi went, the star they had seen in the East shone brightly. "There it is!" they said. And the star's light glowed especially bright on one particular house.

The wise men stopped and got down off their camels. One of them knocked on the door.

Mary opened the door.

Inside the Magi saw a little boy, just able to stand beside his mother. Then the Magi got down on their knees and bowed down to Him. Jesus looked like other boys. But the wise men knew. Jesus was the Son of God.

Now the wise men got out the gifts they had selected so carefully. They hoped their gifts would show how thankful they were to God for the gift of His Son, Jesus.

One wise man opened his treasure box and gave Jesus a gift of gold.

One wise man opened his treasure box, and gave Jesus a gift of very expensive perfume, called incense.

One wise man opened his treasure box, and gave Jesus a gift of expensive spice, called myrrh.

How thrilled and happy the Magi were to be able to give gifts to Jesus, to show their thanks to God.

The wise men didn't go back and report to Herod.

God warned them in a dream to go back to their homes a different way. When the angry Herod heard, he sent soldiers to Bethlehem to search for and kill the baby Jesus.

But before the soldiers got there, an angel came and told Joseph in a dream to hurry to Egypt. Joseph and Mary had been very poor. But with the rich gifts that the Magi gave Mary and Joseph there would be plenty of money now. They used it to hurry with Jesus to safety. God used the Magi's "thank you" Christmas gifts in a very special way.

> ***Action Idea*** This Christmas make your own treasure
> chests, in which to save loose coins or other money for
> a special "thank you" gift for Jesus next Christmas.

Jesus Sees Nathanael
John 1:29–49

What do you suppose is behind the hill?

Background   One of the wonderful realities taught in Scripture is that God is omnipresent. God is able to be in all places at the same time, totally aware of each of us as individuals. God's promise, "I am with you always," is one of the great heritages you and I are able to pass on to our boys and girls.

One of the men who preached God's Word when Jesus was alive in those days was named John the Baptist. John knew that soon God's own Son would come. So John went all around the country telling people to get ready. John didn't know who God's Son was. But John knew that He was coming.

One day John saw Jesus, and God told John, "Jesus is the One!" John was so excited, he couldn't keep the news to himself. "Look," John said to some friends, "this is the One I was talking about. Jesus is the Son of God."

Some of the men whom John told ran and asked Jesus if they could spend the day with Him.

One of the men who spent the day with Jesus was named Philip. Philip was excited too. So Philip went to look for his brother Nathanael.

But where could Nathanael be? Philip looked everywhere. He looked around the town. He looked in the valley. He climbed the hills. Finally Philip found Nathanael, resting under a tree, over a hill and out of sight.

"Nathanael!" Philip called excitedly. "Nathanael! We've found Him. The One the Bible promises. Our Savior is Jesus, a man from Nazareth."

Nathanael wasn't excited at all. "Nazareth," Nathanael said. "Why, no one special could come from that little town."

But Philip was sure. "Come and see for yourself," Philip urged his brother. So Nathanael got up and came with Philip. As they came up to Jesus, Jesus looked at Nathanael and smiled. "Here is a good man," Jesus said. "Here is an honest and faithful person." Nathanael was shocked. How did Jesus know him?[1]

Nathanael couldn't understand how Jesus could know him, to say nice things about him. Nathanael didn't know that Jesus was the Son of God. And God sees everyone, all the time.

"Nathanael," Jesus answered, "I saw you while you were still sitting under the fig tree, before Philip called you."

[1]*How do you suppose Jesus knew the kind of person Nathanael was? Do you think Nathanael liked being called a good person? How do you feel when mom or dad or someone else praises you?*

155

And then Nathanael knew.

Jesus had seen him.

Jesus knew what Nathanael was doing, even when Nathanael was out of sight. Only God can see us always. So Nathanael knew Jesus must be God.

So Nathanael said, "Teacher, You are the Son of God. You are the King of Israel."[2]

God didn't watch Nathanael to catch him doing something wrong. God watched Nathanael to see all the good choices Nathanael made. And Jesus was pleased with Nathanael. Jesus called Nathanael a truly good person.

Jesus sees you and me, and is very pleased with us when we make right choices as Nathanael did. When we have a hard decision to make, it helps to remember Jesus is watching. We can please Jesus by choosing the right thing.[3]

[2]*How do you suppose it made Nathanael feel to know that Jesus always saw him? How do you feel when you think about Jesus seeing you always? (Share how the sense of God's presence makes you feel.)*

[3]*What are some times when it's hard for you to choose to do right—times when mom and dad aren't there to see you? Let's thank God that He is there to watch you. Jesus is always happy with you when you do the right thing to please Him.*

> **Action Idea** It may be fun and helpful to your children if your whole family joins "Club Nathanael." There is only one rule for club members. When they are away from each other, they will remember to do what will please Jesus, who is always with them.
>
> You may find it helpful to your boys and girls to have one or two club meetings a week for a month or two. Let your children make up a club motto, choose a club password in the John 1 passage, and work up a meeting agenda. One feature of the club meeting should be a report of times when remembering that Jesus sees us helped a member make a choice he believes pleased God.

Jesus Heals an Official's Son

John 4:43–54

What would the father do if he couldn't bring his sick boy to Jesus?

Background   Going to the hospital is difficult enough for many adults. It's especially hard for children, who may be even more anxious if they have to be separated from their parents. Telling and talking about this Bible story may minister God's comfort to your children.

The Gospels report many miracles of healing performed by Jesus during His time on earth. Often Jesus' acts of compassion and love carry distinctive touches. The story told of the healing of a royal official's son in John 4 is such an incident. The distinctive here is one of distance. The father of the sick child traveled from his home in Capernaum to Cana to seek Jesus' help. Although the father begged Jesus to come with him, the Lord refused. Instead, Jesus simply promised the boy would be well. The man trusted Jesus' word and turned back toward home. On the way he was met with good news. At the very moment Jesus spoke with him, the child began to recover. Distance and separation were unable to limit the loving, healing touch of God.

Children today will find comfort in the realization that even when parents are not there, God is with them. And God is able to make them well.

157

The worried father walked back and forth. His forehead was wrinkled, and he rubbed his hands together nervously. His son was very sick. But the father wasn't there with him. Even worse, the father knew if he were there, he wouldn't be able to help. What could he do to help his sick boy?

As the father walked back and forth, he noticed excited people outside. They were talking loudly and waving their hands. He could hear them shout joyfully to their friends. It sounded like . . . yes, it was! They were saying that Jesus was coming into town!

The father knew about Jesus. Everyone had heard about Jesus! Why, Jesus went from town to town and taught people about God. And the father knew something else, too. Jesus had made sick people well!

How excited the father felt then. Here was something he could do for his son. The father could ask Jesus to come to his home in Capernaum! Quickly the father hurried out the door and followed the crowds. The father would talk to Jesus, and get Jesus to help!

When the father found Jesus, he rushed up to him. "Jesus," the father begged. "Please come and heal my son. I'm afraid he will die if You don't help!"

Jesus shook His head. "Can't you trust Me unless you see Me perform a miracle?" Jesus asked.

But the father only cared about one thing. "Sir," he said to Jesus, "please come down to my home before my child dies."

Jesus smiled at the man. "It's all right. You can go home now. Your son will live."

The father believed Jesus.

Jesus wasn't there in the room with the sick son. But the father believed that Jesus could make his child well wherever Jesus might be. Relieved and happy, the father started back toward Capernaum. While he was still on the way, some servants met him with the good news. His boy was alive and getting well! When the father asked when the boy got better, the servants told him. It was just the time that Jesus had said, "Your son will live."

How glad the father was that he had talked with Jesus about his son. How glad the father was that Jesus could heal his son, even when the father wasn't there and when Jesus was in Cana, too. Jesus is with us *wherever* we are. And Jesus will help us as He helped the father of the sick boy.

> ***Action Idea*** Rather than talk with your child to help him develop his own insights from this story, use it as a basis to explain your relationship with him or her while in the hospital. You may not be able to be there, just as the father in the story couldn't be with his sick child. But like the father, you will be thinking about your child.
>
> Like the father in the story, you will talk with Jesus to ask His help. You will pray for your child while he's in the hospital. You will visit when you can. But you know that Jesus will be with your child whenever you can't be there. You also trust Jesus to take care of your child and work through the doctors to make him or her well.

Jesus Touches a Leper
Mark 1:40–45

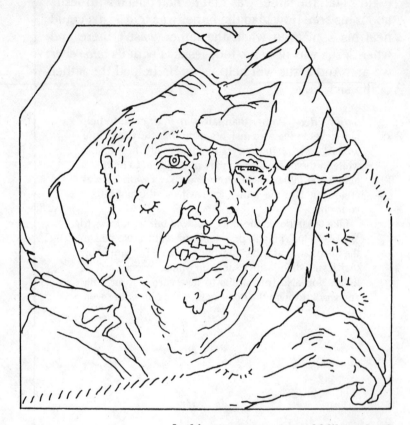

Is this a person you would like to hug?

Background One of the most basic skills children need to develop is the ability to sense what others feel.

The sensitivity of Jesus to the inner needs of individuals, as well as to their more obvious problems, is one of the most attractive features of this Gospel's portrait of our Lord. As you share the story of Jesus healing the leper, as reported in the first chapter of Mark, you can help your boys and girls sense the importance of being aware of other's feelings.

160

Jesus got up very early one morning. He left the house where He was staying and found a place where He could be alone. There Jesus prayed, talking with God the Father.

When Jesus' disciples found Him, they were upset. "Everyone is looking for You, Jesus!" they said.

But Jesus shook His head.

"It's time to go on," Jesus said. "I must go to other towns where people need me. I have to teach them about God. And there are people who hurt, whom I want to help."[1]

As Jesus traveled from town to town, He helped many people who were hurting. One of them was a man with the disease of leprosy.

Leprosy was a terrible disease in Bible times. We don't have much leprosy in our country. But people who had leprosy then suffered very much. Their bodies had great sores on them. Some lepers found their fingers and toes and even ears became very dry and hard. Then the ends of the fingers and toes wore away.

Everyone was afraid of leprosy in Bible days. No one would come near a leper. Everyone was terrified he might get the sickness too.

When the leper came to Jesus, he didn't get close to Him. Instead the leper crawled up and begged Jesus on his knees. "Please," the leper sobbed, "if You are willing, You can make me whole and well again."[2]

Jesus looked at the leper. He knew how much the leper's body hurt. But Jesus knew the leper was hurting inside too. For years no one had loved the leper. No one had touched him. No one had hugged the leper, or told the leper that he was loved. The leper was so lonely, without a single friend, that he hurt deeply inside.

Jesus knew how much the leper hurt inside. Jesus cared very much for the leper, because He understood how he felt.[3]

Jesus knew how much the leper hurt inside. Jesus knew how alone and friendless the leper felt. The leper needed to have his disease healed. But Jesus knew the

[1]What do you suppose were some of the hurts Jesus wanted to help people with? Can you think of ways you have hurt this last week? Do you have any friends who have been hurting this week?

[2]What do you suppose Jesus will do? How do you think Jesus felt about the leper? Do you think the leper is one of the hurting people Jesus wanted to help? Where do you think the leper hurt most?

[3]Do you ever hurt inside? What happened to make you feel hurt inside? Can you name some of the feelings that you had when you hurt inside?

161

leper also needed to be loved. "I am willing," Jesus told him. "Be well." And Jesus did something else. He reached out and touched the lonely leper, to heal the hurt inside.

When Jesus touched the leper, and his sickness was healed, the man knew that someone loved him. The leper would not have to be lonely any more.[4]

[4]How do you think Jesus knew the leper hurt inside? How can we tell when someone is lonely, or hurts inside in some other way? What helps you when you hurt inside?

Action Idea Make a list of all the words your children can think of that describe unhappy or hurting feelings. Write each feeling on a 3 X 5 card. You might want to make this a family project, to last a week. Have each family member keep looking for new feeling words to add to your cards. Words may show up in reading, or older boys and girls may look in a dictionary.

When you have a complete list, you can use the cards in a number of ways. You may make a game for the family to play. Each person draws a card at random. Then he or she tries to act out the feelings, so others will guess how he feels inside. The acting can be pantomime. Or you may use words. When the family has guessed the inside feeling, each can (a) tell of a time he or she felt that way and what happened to bring on the feeling, or (b) suggest ways to help a person with those feelings.

The goal of this family game is to help your children recognize clues to others' feelings by their behavior. Practice can help them become more sensitive to others, learn how to put themselves in others' places and respond with Christlike compassion to others' needs.

Jesus Calms the Storm
Matthew 8:23–27

When was the last time you were this afraid?

Background The children in my Sunday school class were drawing pictures to show what they liked best about this Bible story. Most of them picked dramatic themes. They drew great waves and a tossing boat. Or they drew Jesus standing in the boat, with His arms raised to calm the storm. But one nine-year-old drew a very different picture. She drew a picture of a room, with a bed and window, and in the window she showed a quarter moon.

When I asked her to tell me about the picture, she explained.

"What I like best is that at night, when I'm afraid of the dark, I remember that Jesus is with me like He was with His disciples in the boat."

Fears are very real to boys and girls. But the sense of Jesus' presence can bring an inner calm into their lives. When Jesus is present, life is not out of control. Jesus is able to calm our storms as well.

Jesus was very tired, there on the lakeshore. Jesus had been teaching the people of Israel about God for hours and hours. And still more people came, wanting to hear Jesus, and hoping Jesus would help the sick get well.

Finally Jesus had to leave the crowd that pressed around Him to go to another place. He got into a boat with His disciples, and they pushed the boat out into the big lake.

Jesus was so tired He fell asleep right away.

The disciples put up the sail. Probably the disciples tried to be very quiet. They didn't want to wake Jesus up.

But as the boat got out into the middle of the lake, a terrible wind began to blow. Suddenly, without any warning at all, giant waves began to toss the little boat.

Jesus' disciples were fishermen. They had spent most of their lives working in boats on this lake. But this storm was the worst one they had ever seen. Before long the disciples were sure the boat was going to sink. Water from the high waves was splashing in, and the boat was about to fill with water.

Jesus was still asleep!

Finally the disciples cried out in terror. Shaking Jesus to wake Him up, they said, "Lord, save us! We're about to drown!"[1]

The disciples were very afraid.

But when Jesus woke up, He was surprised.

"Why are you so afraid?" Jesus asked them. "Don't you trust Me?" The disciples should have known that nothing could hurt them, because Jesus was with them.

Jesus stood up in the tossing boat.

Jesus looked at the waves and felt the howling winds. He looked at the wild waters. Then Jesus said, "Stop!" Immediately the wind was still. Immediately the waves stopped tossing. Immediately the lake was completely calm.[2]

The disciples were amazed. They had never dreamed that Jesus could even make the storm, the winds, and the waves obey Him.

[1] *(Give each family member a sheet of paper and crayons. Have each person draw a picture of the disciples' faces when they saw how terrible the storm was.) Let's talk about our pictures. How do you think the disciples felt in that boat? How did you show that feeling in your picture? Do you remember ever feeling the way the disciples felt? Tell us about when you felt afraid.*

[2] *How do you think the men with Jesus felt then? Why would they have those feelings?*

164

The disciples were learning just how wonderful Jesus is. When Jesus was with them, the disciples would never need to be afraid.[3]

> **Action Idea** Continue to use drawings to help your children apply this story to their own fears. Have each family member draw a picture of a time when he or she is glad that Jesus is with him, as Jesus was with the men in the boat. If your children need help, remind them of times they mentioned when you did the first *talkable* together.

[3]*Draw a picture of what you like best about this story. Tell us about your picture, and why you drew what you did.*

Jesus' Neighbors Send Him Away

Luke 4:13–30

How do you feel when friends won't let you play?

Background Children are often unthinkingly cruel to one another. One day girls are best friends. The next day one won't play with or even talk with another. Or the neighborhood boys run off to play, leaving your son out. "You can't come. It's just for our club!" is a phrase which makes club membership seem special to those who are in—but can deeply hurt those left out.

You can use this Bible story of Jesus' rejection by his neighbors in his home town to help your children explore their feelings when rejected. The *talkables* are designed on the assumption that talking about what has happened will help your boy or girl to be better able to handle rejection experiences.

166

Jesus was famous now.

All over the land of Israel, people talked about Jesus. People were amazed at what Jesus taught them about God. People were amazed at the miracles Jesus did to help others. Everyone was sure that Jesus was very special.[1]

Of course, Jesus was more special than anyone who ever lived. Jesus was God's own Son. And Jesus came to show the people of the world how much God loves them. People who were sure that Jesus is special were right.

And then Jesus came to His hometown.

Jesus was born in Bethlehem, but His family moved and settled in Nazareth. Jesus lived in Nazareth for years and years, and worked there as a carpenter. Nazareth was a small town, so Jesus knew almost everyone. And everyone knew Jesus.

All Jesus' neighbors had heard about the wonderful things Jesus was doing in Israel. That weekend, everyone was in the synagogue-church when Jesus came.

How curious they were.

What would Jesus do?

Well, that morning Jesus got up and read from the Bible. He read a part of the Bible that told about His own coming to be our Savior. Jesus' neighbors listened. But they weren't happy about what Jesus said. Instead they resented Jesus.

"Who does Jesus think He is?" someone muttered.

"Yeah," another one said, "He's not *that* special. Why, Jesus is just one of a poor carpenter's family. He can't be important."

"We know Jesus' brothers and His sisters," someone else spoke up. "Why, Jesus' brothers, James and Joseph and Simon and Judas, are just plain people, like us. Who does Jesus think He is anyway?"

Jesus' friends and neighbors were actually getting angry at Him! Jesus' friends didn't seem to like Him at all![2]

[1]*Can you name some people who think you are special? (Be sure to share ways in which your child is special to you. Also encourage your child to name friends who may think he or she is special too.) How does it make you feel to know that others like you and think you are special?*

[2]*Have your friends or neighbors ever been angry at you without a good reason? Tell about a time when your friends decided they didn't like you. How did you feel when your friends did that? Why do you think they were angry or didn't like you?*

167

[3]Do your friends ever chase you away and not want to play with you? How do you feel when that happens? What do you suppose Jesus will do now? How will He feel?

Jesus must have felt particularly sad when all His friends and neighbors got up and tried to chase Him out of town! "Go away!" they yelled. Some of them were even ready to throw stones at Jesus, or throw Jesus down to hurt Him. But God took care of Jesus, as He takes care of us.[3]

Jesus knew that He couldn't be with His friends when they didn't want Him. So Jesus went on to another town, and He began to teach there. Jesus knew that He was special; even if His friends didn't like Him then. Jesus would keep on loving others. Someday many of His old friends would believe in Him, and like Him again.[4]

[4]Can you think of times when your friends didn't want to play one day, but wanted to play with you the next day? If you and I keep on being friendly, our friends will usually want to be with us again soon.

Action Idea Make a "rejection wheel" from a paper plate divided into equal pie-shaped segments. Each segment can be labeled as illustrated. The plate can be colored by the child to show how he or she feels at each stage, and thumbtacked to a wall or bulletin board. If you wish, also tack a pointer in the upper right quadrant, and let your child rotate the plate through the cycle as he or she experiences times of rejection. Your goal in making the Rejection Wheel is to help your child have a sense of hope when he or she hurts, knowing that the one who rejected will be a friend again soon.

Jesus, the Good Shepherd
John 10

The good shepherd sleeps in the open gate, so no wild animal can get to his sheep.

Background Nighttime fears are so common with boys and girls of six to eight and even older that several stories in this book are designed to provide a sense of nighttime security.

This very simple story builds on Jesus' presentation of Himself in John 10 as the Good Shepherd. It is designed to help children understand what Bible-time boys and girls knew, and will help our children feel the wonderful peace which comes when we know that Jesus shepherds us.

169

Everyone knew about sheep and shepherds.

Yes, everyone listening to Jesus talk knew just how shepherds took care of their sheep. When people heard Jesus tell them that He is the Good Shepherd, everyone would have known that Jesus was promising to take care of them.[1]

At night in Bible times, shepherds kept their sheep in a safe pen. Some pens were made of thorn bushes, with sharp spikes to keep wild animals and robbers out. Inside the sheep would be safe.

The pen for the sheep had only one gate. At night, when the sheep were safe inside, the shepherd didn't leave them alone. He closed the gate with more thorn bushes. And then the shepherd lay down to sleep right by the door. No one could come in to hurt the sheep. The shepherd guarded the sheep at night. The shepherd was there to keep them safe.

Jesus said, "I am the gate." Jesus is our Shepherd, and He protects us. Jesus takes care of us at night and in the daytime. Jesus is always with us to keep us safe.[2]

Good shepherds loved their sheep. They would do anything to protect them. A good shepherd would fight wild animals to save one of his sheep. Even when the shepherd might be hurt or killed, the good shepherd would fight a lion or a bear or a wolf.

Jesus wanted people to know how much He loves us. So Jesus said, "I am the Good Shepherd. The Good Shepherd lays down His life for His sheep." Jesus loved you and me so much He died on the cross to pay for our sins. Jesus proved then how much He loves us. Because we are Jesus' sheep, we can know that He loves us always.

God wants you and me to know always that Jesus loves us. Jesus is our Good Shepherd. Jesus keeps us safe at night. He knows everything about us, and is with us always. Jesus loves us very, very much.

Action Idea A number of reassuring activities can grow out of this simple survey of what it means to have

[1] What do you know about sheep and their shepherds? What do shepherds do that makes sheep feel safe? What do you suppose shepherds do at night that makes sheep feel safe in the dark? When Jesus told us He is the Good Shepherd, He did it so we could always feel safe, too.

[2] Let me tell you about a time I was glad Jesus was with me as my Shepherd [share]. When do you most want Jesus to shepherd you?

Jesus as our Good Shepherd. For instance, you might learn the familiar chorus, "His Sheep Am I," and sing it with the children at bedtime. You might find a picture of Jesus as the Good Shepherd at a Christian bookstore for your child's room. Another simple but very helpful project is to memorize the Shepherd's Psalm, Psalm 23, as a family project.

Shepherds carried a long staff with a hook in one end. The heavy wood let them fight off wild animals. And the hook at the end let them reach down and rescue sheep that had fallen into a deep ditch. Can you tell how the hook would help?

The Good Samaritan
Luke 10:25–37

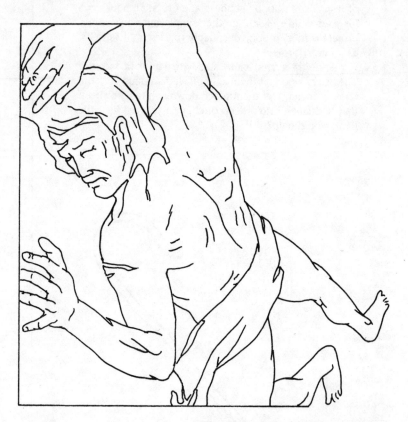

Would you stop to help this man?

Background The story of the Good Samaritan is one of the most familiar in the Bible. It is penetrating, because it cuts through all the differences which divide human beings. The Good Samaritan shows clearly God's concern that we love and have compassion for others. Although the story was told to point up the failure of those religious people who looked for ways to release themselves from the obligation to care, the Good Samaritan has been especially precious to Jesus' followers. How clearly we sense God's call to us to identify with others in their need, and to reach out with help.

172

It was dangerous to travel in Bible times. A traveler might meet wild animals out in the country. Robbers might be hiding alongside the road, looking for a chance to steal from someone who was alone. So perhaps one man whom Jesus told about had a special reason to hurry along the road between Jerusalem and Jericho. He was hurrying. And he was alone.

And then it happened!

Robbers jumped out from behind some rocks. The robbers grabbed the traveler and beat him. They took all his money. They took the packages he was carrying. They even took all his clothes. Then the robbers hit the man some more and left him lying along the side of the road.

The man moaned and tried to move.

But he couldn't move. He was hurt too badly. All the man could do was lie there on the rocky road, while the hot sun burned his bruised skin.[1]

The traveler lay there in the hot sun. He couldn't help himself. And how he hurt! Then he heard someone coming. Maybe the person would help him. The hurt traveler couldn't even lift his head to look. But he did see feet walking along the road.

The man who was walking by was a priest. When the priest saw the hurt man lying there, with no clothes at all and great bruises on his body, the priest didn't stop. Instead the priest looked around fearfully. Maybe the robbers were still near! Instead of stopping, the priest crossed all the way to the other side of the road, and walked around the hurt traveler. When the priest was past him, he hurried away down the road.[2]

The hurt traveler lay there in the hot sun. He seemed to hurt even more. And then the hurt man heard more footsteps.

When this man saw the hurt traveler, he went to the other side of the road, too. He hurried by the hurt man, trying hard to look in another direction.[3]

The third man to come by was a Samaritan, a man from the country right next to Israel. The people of

[1]What words can you think of that might tell how the hurt man feels? Have you ever known anyone who might feel hurt (use the words your children might have suggested)?

[2]How do you suppose the hurt man felt when the priest went by? Do you think you would like that priest for a friend? Why, or why not? What kind of person would you like as a friend?

[3]What do you think the men who passed by should have done? Was it a good thing to look away and hurry by the hurt man? Why, or why not? How do you and I act when we notice someone who is crying, or looking sad, or maybe is being laughed at by others? How do you suppose we might help?

173

[4]Would you like your friends to be like the Samaritan? How can friends be like him? Can you think of any time when you've been a good Samaritan, and thought about how others might feel?

Israel and the Samaritans didn't like each other. But this Samaritan didn't ask what country the hurt man came from. Instead the Samaritan went right up to the hurt man. He bandaged the hurt man's wounds, put oil on his sunburn, and gave him a drink. Then he helped the hurt man up, and supported him as the hurt man sat on the Samaritan's own donkey. Down the trail the two went. And when they came to an inn, the Samaritan got a room for the hurt Israelite. The Samaritan sat up with him that night and took care of him. When the Samaritan had to leave the next day, he gave money to the innkeeper. "Take good care of the hurt man," the Samaritan said. "If you have to spend more money than this to help him, I will pay you when I come back to your inn."[4]

Jesus looked around at the people to whom He was telling this story. "Who was a good friend and neighbor to the man who was robbed?" Jesus asked. One of Jesus' listeners said, "The one who had mercy on him."

Jesus nodded His head. And then Jesus told the man the same thing the Bible tells us.

"Go," Jesus said, "and be just like the Good Samaritan."

Action Idea If your congregation participates in the collection of food for the needy at Thanksgiving or Christmas, do more this year than bring cans to the church. Take your children and participate in delivering the food to the families for which it is intended.

Afterward, talk about the experience and how your family can best share the many blessings you have received from the Lord.

Jesus Visits Mary and Martha

Luke 10:38–42

What do you think is important to Martha?

Background Perhaps the most important thing we learn is that our children are individuals, as were Mary and Martha. They have different personalities and values. These differences will give rise to conflicts, and we need God's own gift of wisdom not to take sides with one child against the other. Rather we need to help each boy or girl understand himself and his siblings.

175

" **J** esus is coming!"

Mary rushed into the kitchen to tell her sister, Martha. "I just heard, Martha," Mary said. "Jesus is coming to visit us tomorrow."

When Mary had told Martha, Mary hurried out to give the news to other friends. Mary was that kind of person. She liked to be with people. She liked to talk with them, and listen, and sometimes Mary just liked to sit and look at the sky and think how wonderful God's sunsets are.

When Mary had gone, though, Martha started planning. *Now,* Martha thought, *what will I feed Jesus for supper? It's got to be very special. Maybe I should try that new recipe. . . .* Before you knew it, Martha had a list of all the things she needed to do before Jesus came. Martha was thinking where to go to borrow the extra dishes to feed Jesus' disciples, what to buy to cook for them, what time she'd need to get up to do everything, and many, many other things. Martha was already beginning to feel a little worried and anxious. How could she ever get everything done![1]

Mary and Martha were sisters. But they were very different from each other. That's really all right. Each person is special. God doesn't mind if we're different.

But sometimes the differences between Mary and Martha got the two sisters into trouble. They loved each other, of course. But because they were different, Mary and Martha didn't always understand each other.

For instance, Mary probably helped Martha get the house ready for Jesus' visit. She probably dusted and cleaned, and helped prepare the food to be cooked. But when Jesus came, Mary was so excited. She just wanted to be near Jesus and listen to everything Jesus taught. So Mary slipped out of the kitchen and sat down on the floor near Jesus to listen.

Martha was working in the hot kitchen. She had four or five things she was trying to cook, and all Martha could think about was that Mary wouldn't help.

Martha burst into the living room where Jesus and

[1]*Which of the two sisters are you most like? Mary, who just lets things happen and spends lots of time talking or thinking? Or are you like Martha, who plans work and is very responsible? What do you think mom is most like? Dad? Why? What are some other ways people in our family are different from each other?*

Mary and the others were sitting, and she complained to Jesus. "Lord," Martha said, "don't You care that my sister has left me to do all the work by myself? Tell her to help me!"[2]

Martha knew how she felt. Martha was worried about the dinner, and frustrated because there were so many things to do. Martha felt sorry for herself, and angry at Mary—all at the same time! It was so important to Martha to have a fancy dinner for Jesus, she couldn't think of anything else.

But the dinner with all the special foods wasn't that important to Mary. What was important to Mary was to spend as much time as she could with Jesus. Mary wanted to be with Jesus, not be in some hot kitchen. How terrible it would be if Jesus visited, and Mary didn't have any time to be with Him because she was cooking.[3]

Jesus heard Martha complain. And Jesus listened when Martha said, "Lord, make my sister come help me."

But Jesus shook His head. Jesus wouldn't make Mary do what Martha thought was important. Mary had a right to choose for herself what she thought was important to her. And Mary was sure that sitting there, to listen to Jesus, was very important indeed.

"Martha," Jesus said, "you're all upset about so many things. Really, I didn't come here because of what you cook for Me, but to be with you. You could just give Me a plate of beans—just that one thing—and I'd be happy. This time Mary made the better choice, and I won't take away her chance to spend time with Me just because cooking is so important to you."[4]

It's not wrong to be different, and have different things be important to us. When we feel angry and upset, as Martha did, we need to talk about things with our family. Maybe we can find ways to help each other, and we surely can think about what things in our lives are most important to God.

Action Idea   When conflicts develop it's important to help each child talk about what is important to him or her in the situation.

[2]*What do you think Jesus will tell Martha? Why? Can you think of the last time you complained to mom or dad about your brother (sister)? What was it about? How did you feel when you complained about your brother (sister)?*

[3]*What do you think about that? Which was most important? To cook a fancy dinner, or to spend time with Jesus? Why? When sisters or brothers like Mary and Martha get upset with each other, it's because they have different ideas about what is important.*

[4]*How do you suppose Martha felt when Jesus explained? Do you think Martha learned? What can you and I learn about how to get along better with our brothers (sisters)?*

To help develop this skill, role play Mary and Martha getting ready for Jesus' visit. In the spontaneous conversation, have each character say what is important to her, and try to explain why. After the two sisters have talked, then think together how they might have helped each other, so each gets her important things done. For instance, Mary might have agreed to do certain things *until* Jesus arrived. And Martha might have agreed that she would cook fewer foods, and plan things so Mary could spend time with Jesus—and perhaps so Martha herself could too!

Use this same role play approach to act out ways to handle common conflicts between your children.

Jesus Teaches About Prayer

Luke 11:1–13

How would Jesus tell her to pray?

Background All boys and girls who have loving, approachable fathers will quickly transfer the feeling of closeness and confidence to relationship with the Lord. Boys and girls with inconsistent dads, or those in single-parent homes, may hear mixed messages in Jesus' affirmation that God is a good Father. This Bible story is retold with Jesus' own stress: a stress that helps each of us realize that God is our Father, and that God is the best Father anyone could possibly be.

179

Jesus' disciples were confused.

Many religious people in Israel prayed in special ways. Some stood on street corners and prayed out loud. Others came to the temple-church and raised their arms toward the heavens. Some stood and prayed by quoting verses from the Bible. But Jesus didn't seem to do any of these things.

Sometimes Jesus got up early and went outside to pray alone. Sometimes Jesus prayed and thanked God for helping Him heal people. Jesus' prayers were very simple—just like talking with God.

The disciples watched Jesus for a long time.

Finally the disciples went to Jesus after He finished praying in a quiet place in the country. "Jesus," the disciples said, "will You teach us how to pray?"

Jesus nodded His head yes.

Jesus must have been pleased. Jesus knew that God likes us to pray and talk with Him. And Jesus knew that His disciples needed to learn to talk with God.

So Jesus nodded His head. Yes, Jesus was glad to teach people how to pray.[1]

The most important thing Jesus wanted His disciples to know was this: God loves us very much. When we pray, we do not talk to a God who is a stranger. Oh, no. So Jesus said, when you pray, begin by saying "Father."

Now, not every human father is a good father. Jesus wanted us to know that God is a very good Father. So Jesus told a story.

"Suppose," Jesus said, "you have visitors come, and you need extra food. It's late, but you go next door and knock on your neighbor's door."

"Go away!" the neighbor says. "Stop knocking! I've gone to bed."

Jesus explained. "If it's just a neighbor, you may have to keep on knocking and knocking until finally the neighbor gets up just to keep you from bothering him.

"Well, God isn't like that. God is a good Father. A good father listens to you the very first time, because he loves you."

[1] *Do you ever wonder about praying, as the disciples did? Why do you suppose people pray? What do you think people ought to talk with God about? When do you best like to pray?*

180

So when you and I pray, and we say "Father" to God, it's because we know that He loves us. We know that God hears us the very first time we pray.[2]

Jesus wants everyone to know when he or she prays that God is the very best Father there could be.

Action Idea Look with your children at how Jesus taught His disciples to pray. The following is Luke's version of the Lord's Prayer, with simple observations on key phrases which you can talk over with your children:

The Prayer:	Insights:
Father	We know when we pray that God loves us and will listen to us.
hallowed be your name	God is special. When we pray we can praise Him, and tell Him how glad we are for who He is.
Your kingdom come	Someday everyone will do what God says is good and right. When we pray we can ask God to help us obey, as good citizens of God's kingdom.
Give us each day our daily bread	Whatever we need each day, God wants us to tell Him about. God loves us and will give us what we need.
Forgive us our sins	God wants us to confess our sins when we do wrong. God will forgive us. And God wants us to forgive others who sin against us.
Lead us not into temptation	We can ask God to help us be stronger than any temptation, and help us do what is right. We do not need to give in and do wrong.

[2] *What are some things a bad father might do, or might not do? What are some things a good father will do, or will not do? (Make lists of good/poor father qualities.) What do you think is the most important thing about a good father? (Be sure to include your own thoughts on the list, and share your ideas of important father qualities.)*

Jesus Tells About a
Rich Fool
Luke 12:13–21

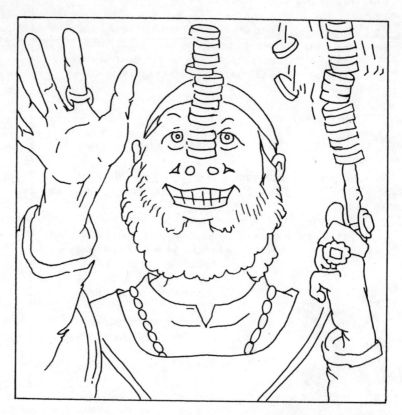

How can you be rich and not smart?

Background We live in a materialistic culture. It isn't surprising if our children show an unhealthy concentration on possessions at times—or if we are pulled in that direction ourselves.

One story which Jesus told His listeners focuses on the foolishness of materialism. In bold, graphic words Jesus described a rich man who thought the meaning of his life was summed up in his abundant possessions. He was wrong. Relationship with God is the basic issue in life, and the rich fool had ignored this relationship.

"Well, sir," the farm manager said, "I just don't know where we're going to put it all."

The rich man didn't say anything. He just frowned, pretending to be angry with the manager.

Shaking a little bit, because the rich man was very, very rich, the manager said, "You see, sir, you've got so many flocks and so many tons and tons of grain from the last harvest, your barns just won't hold it all. You must be the richest farmer in all of Israel."

Inside the rich man smiled. But outside, he kept on frowning. "Well then," the rich man said harshly, "go tear down the barns that are too small. Build bigger ones. Build the biggest barns in all Israel! Build them big enough to store all the many things I own." The rich man shook his fist at the manager. "Go on, now, and do it in a hurry!"

When the farm manager had gone, the smile the rich man had been hiding came out. The rich man leaned back in his chair. He smiled and smiled. Now and then he laughed too.[1]

It's not wrong to be rich, or to own many things. But when a person cares too much about his possessions, there are important things he can forget.

That was the problem with the rich man. He sat there when the manager had gone, and smiled. And he talked to himself. "I'm a lucky person. I have plenty of good things, all laid up for many years. I can take it easy now. I can eat, and drink, and have parties for years and years and years."

The rich man was thinking only about himself, and he thought that his riches would make him happy.[2]

The rich man in Jesus' story had forgotten all about God and what was important to God. All the rich man ever thought about was his money and the things he owned.

The rich man felt very happy that afternoon. He smiled, and now and then he laughed when he thought about the years and years of parties and the riches he would have.

[1]*Do you suppose you would have liked to be the rich man? Why, or why not? What might be some good things about being rich? What do you think might be bad things about being rich? Do you think the farm manager liked the rich man? Why or why not?*

[2]*Have you ever felt that there was something you needed that, if you got it, would make you happy for a long time? Tell us about it. Did you get it, and how long did it make you feel happy? (If you didn't get it, how long did not having it make you feel unhappy?) What do you think helps a person be really happy?*

The Bible tells us how to be really happy. We can try to please God, rather than just think about what we will get. Being rich in God's way means caring about other people, helping them because we love God.

The rich man was very happy all evening. He smiled even more, and began to plan what he would do first to enjoy his riches.

But that night, the rich man died.

And God said to him, "You are a fool. What good do you think all the things you own will do you now?"[3]

God doesn't want any of us to make the mistake of thinking that the things we have or want are most important. Things are never more important than wanting to please God.

[3] Why do you suppose Jesus ended His story this way? The rich man stored up all he owned to use for himself. What do you think he could have done with some of the things he owned that would have been wiser?

Action Idea   Hold a family evaluation. How do each of us show that pleasing God is important to us? How do we use our money or other possessions to show that we care about other people? Areas like use of allowances, sharing of some toys, and so on, can all be discussed.

After the evaluation, family members might each try to express one way in which each will seek to better use possessions to please the Lord.

Jesus Talks About God's Love

Luke 12:22–34

Who wins the "best dressed" contest?

Background This Bible story is a companion to the preceding story of the rich fool. Through the former story, Jesus wanted His listeners to understand that the meaning of life is not found in luxuries. Through this story, Jesus wants His followers to learn the stunning truth that we need not even worry about necessities. The point, of course, is that it's not only the rich who are materialistic. The poor may be materialistic too. At heart, materialism is nothing less than acting as if the material universe were the totality of reality, and failing to grasp spiritual realities.

185

Jesus was sitting with His disciples.

The disciples were people who trusted Jesus, and who followed Him. The disciples were Jesus' friends, just as you and I are friends who love Jesus and want to please Him.

Sitting there, close to Jesus, the disciples heard Jesus say, "You don't have to worry." Jesus told them, "You don't have to be afraid."[1]

Jesus loves His disciples very much. Jesus loves you and me. So He told two stories to help us know just how much God loves us, and why we don't have to worry or be afraid.

"I tell you," Jesus began, "don't worry about what you will have to eat or what clothes you'll have to wear. You are very important, and very special, and that's why you don't need to worry.

"Just look at those birds flying over there," Jesus said, pointing to some larger birds in a nearby field. "You know, those birds don't work in any field. Those birds don't have barns to store grain. The birds find what they need to eat each day, for God feeds them.

"You know, you are much more special to God than birds. Surely God, who takes care of the birds, will take care of you. God loves you, for you are very special to Him."[2]

Jesus wanted to make sure that His disciples really felt special. So Jesus told them another story.

"Look," Jesus said, pointing out some flowers that were growing in the fields. "See how beautiful these flowers are. You know, those flowers don't worry about what they wear. But God has given them beautiful petals to clothe them. Those petals are more beautiful than the wonderful robes of King Solomon. Now," Jesus went on, "flowers only live for a few days. If God clothes them so beautifully, how much more will God take care of you? You are far more special and important to God than the flowers. So you can trust God, and not be afraid."[3]

[1] *Why do you suppose Jesus told His disciples that? What do you suppose some of these friends of Jesus worried about? What do you suppose they might be afraid of?*

[2] *How do you suppose Jesus' disciples felt when they thought about being special to God? How does it make you feel to know that you are special, and that God loves you very much?*

[3] *Do you suppose Jesus' disciples realized how special they were to God? Just for fun, let's make up some "more special" sayings. For instance, "Jimmy (substitute child's name), you're more special to us and to God than the newest new car." (Let your children make up as many "more special" sayings as they can.)*

Jesus told His disciples these stories so they wouldn't worry or be afraid. Jesus wants each of us to know how special and how important we are to God.

And Jesus knew something else, too.

When we know we're special, and that God is taking care of us, we can also choose to do what pleases God. We know that God will take care of us, so pleasing God is the most important thing in our whole life.

> ***Action Idea*** Younger boys and girls will appreciate a simple picture panel for their room. On the left panel attach a picture of your child's favorite bird. On the right panel attach a picture of a favorite beautiful flower. In the center panel, attach a picture of the child. You may want to print a phrase from Luke 12 on the picture panel. For instance, "How much more valuable you are" (12:24) or "Your Father knows that you need them. . . . Do not be afraid" (12:30, 32).

The Lost Sheep
Matthew 18:10–14

Why would Herbie the sheep want to run away?

Background When our younger children wander away, or "forget" to come home, we do worry. We find them—and express our worry with anger. When our older children stray from godliness, we all too often become bitter and demanding. Yet God always maintains His attitude of amazing grace toward us, who are also so prone to stray.

In this retelling of Jesus' familiar tale of the lost sheep, we want to help our children who run away sense the anguish they cause, and yet be assured of our joy at their return. Because love is a much more powerful motivator than fear, this story can help you encourage your wandering child to think of you the next time he's tempted to go off on an adventure—and to choose not to run away.

One day Jesus told a story that helps us understand how much God loves us. It was a story about a lost sheep. Let's pretend we're watching the flock of sheep that Jesus is telling about. Let's see what we can imagine . . .

The shepherd we're watching has a hundred sheep. That's a lot of sheep to take care of. But the shepherd knows every one of the sheep. In fact, each of the sheep has his own name, and the shepherd knows each one by name (cf. John 10:14). Every single sheep is important to the shepherd, who loves them all.

But sheep are a lot like people. They are different from one another. Some sheep are very obedient. They love the shepherd and always do just what the shepherd says.

Some sheep are obedient, but they forget sometimes. They get curious about things and wander off. When the shepherd calls, they're too busy to come.

Some sheep are very independent. They know the shepherd loves them. But they have a mind of their own. They want to do what they want to do, when they want to do it. What they want to do seems more important to them than how the shepherd might feel.[1]

The shepherd loves all his sheep. Every sheep is important to him, even the ones who don't obey, and the ones who don't listen well, and the ones who sometimes run away. In fact, look—(pretend to point to a wandering sheep)—there goes Herbie the runaway now. He's sneaking away while the shepherd is helping another sheep get a stone out of her hoof. The shepherd doesn't see Herbie. There! Now Herbie is hidden beyond those bushes. The shepherd can't see Herbie now. Look at Herbie run![2]

I'll bet you're right. Herbie is running away again because (fill in your child's reason).

Look. I think the shepherd knows that something is wrong. The shepherd is counting his sheep. One. Two. Three. Four . . . it must take a long time to get all the way to a hundred. (Pause.) Ah. Now the shepherd knows. There are only ninety-nine sheep in his flock. One of them has run away.

[1]*What are the three kinds of sheep in the shepherd's flock? Which kind of sheep do you think you'd like best? Why? If you were a sheep, which of the three would you be most like?*

Which sheep do you think the shepherd loves most? Why do you think so?

[2]*What do you suppose Herbie the runaway is thinking about as he runs away? Why do you suppose Herbie likes to run away so much? What do you think? (Accept whatever reason for running away your child suggests as most likely—and be aware of the insight his opinion gives into his own motivations!)*

The shepherd looks around carefully. Yes, you can see the shepherd knows now what sheep is gone. It's Herbie! Herbie has run away again![3]

You can tell how the shepherd feels by what he's doing. He seems to be very worried. He's hurrying to look at that dangerous cliff. He's afraid something bad has happened to Herbie. Now the shepherd looks very sad. See, there's a tear in his eye. I don't think the shepherd is angry. But the shepherd is very, very worried. It really is terrible when someone you love is lost. You think of the bad things that might happen to him (or her) and feel very upset.

See. The shepherd has decided to go look for Herbie. He's getting all the other sheep together, to make sure they are all right. Now the shepherd is going off to look for Herbie.[4]

Well, the shepherd looked and looked for Herbie. He walked up and down hills. He tore his robe on some bushes. And the shepherd scraped his arm on some sharp rocks, too.

Finally, the shepherd called out gladly. "I've found you. And you're all right!"

The shepherd picked Herbie up in his arms, and headed back to where he had left his flock. All the way the shepherd was very happy. He had found Herbie before Herbie could be hurt or killed by wild animals. Herbie was safe now.[5]

We're worried when you run away, and happy when you come home.

> **Action Idea** One wise thing to do with running away is to delay discussion. Simply bring your child home rejoicing, tuck him or her into bed, tell your child how much you care, and let it go for the moment.
>
> The next day or so, however, you will want to use this Bible story. The goal of the story is to help your child gain insight into how you feel when he or she runs away, and to establish expectations, so that fear will not keep him from returning if he should stray again.

A Dad and a Bad Son
Luke 15:11–24

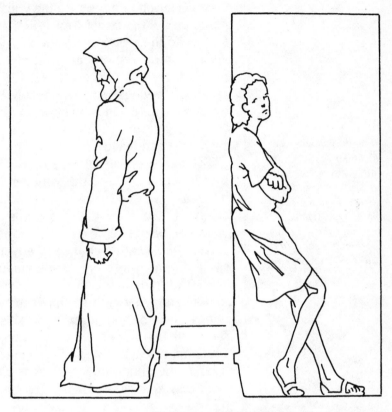

How can a dad and a bad son ever get back together again?

Background The warm, wonderful story of the Prodigal Son has been told and retold to every generation. How clearly we see in it the loving attitude of God our Father, and His eagerness to forgive. How powerfully we sense the welcome awaiting us when we stray from the Lord. Probably no story tells us more beautifully that God is truly ready to forgive.

"Dad, I want to leave home."

Jesus told about the surprising thing the younger son said to his father.

It was surprising because the younger son had a very good family. His father loved him. There was work for him to do in the family business. The younger son had all the food and clothing he needed. And people liked him.

But the younger son had decided. The younger son wanted to leave home. So he went to his father. He said, "Father, give me my share of the family business in cash, so I can leave."[1]

The father loved both his sons. But the father realized he couldn't keep the younger son at home if the boy really wanted to leave. So the father divided up his business, and gave the younger son the money that would be his share.

Excited about his chance to adventure, the younger son left home and went to see distant countries.

But the younger son made some very tragic mistakes. At home the younger son had been taught not to do bad things. Now the son began to do all sorts of bad things. He spent his money on sinful things. And before the young man realized it, all his money was gone!

Well, the younger son thought, *I'll just have to get work and take care of myself.* But things were hard in the far country. The younger son couldn't get a job. Before long he was actually starving!

The younger son looked and looked, and finally he was able to get a job, taking care of a farmer's pigs. But all that the younger son got for his work was a chance to eat the food the pigs were eating. No one was kind to the younger son, or cared about him at all.[2]

Sitting there in the pig pen, the younger son thought about what he had done. He thought about his home. At home, people who worked for his father were given enough to eat. His father's workers were treated kindly. If only he hadn't left home. . . .

And then the younger son had an idea.

[1]How do you suppose the father felt when the younger son wanted to leave? Where and why do you think the son might have wanted to go? What do you think the younger son will do with all his money?

[2]How do you think the younger son felt then? Do you think he was treated fairly—should he have suffered that way for wasting his father's money, and using it wickedly? What do you suppose the father would think if he knew what the younger son did?

I'll get up, the younger son thought, *and I'll go back to my father. I'll tell my father I've sinned, and don't deserve to be treated like a son anymore. I'll ask my father if he will let me work for him as a hired man.*

So the younger son got up and hurried back to his home. It was a long trip. He was very tired and sad when he got home. He thought about his father. He must have wondered what the father would do. *What I really deserve,* the young man must have thought, *is. . . .*[3]

The father saw the son coming a long way off. How happy and excited the father felt. The father didn't wait for the son to come to him. He jumped up and ran to meet his boy.

The younger son tried to apologize. "Father," the son said, "I have sinned, and I'm not worthy of being called your son. . . ."

But the father didn't listen to any more than that. The father didn't listen to the younger son's request to work for him. Instead, the happy father called to his workers. "Quick! Get my son fine clothes. And kill that special calf we're feeding. We're going to have a party. This is my son! He was lost, but now is found. He was dead, and now is alive again!"[4]

> **Action Idea** See if you and the family can locate one or more flat stones, with surfaces as smooth as possible. You can have fun making "prodigal stones" for each person. On one side simply paint the words, "I confess," and on the other, "You're forgiven." Or pick phrases closer to the words of the story, such as, "Father, I have sinned" for one side, and on the other side, "Welcome home."
>
> These stones can be carried as reminders of the fact that when we do sin, we can confess and know that God will forgive us.

[3] *What do you think the young man really deserves? Why? How do you suppose the father will greet him? Will the father feel glad to see the son, or be angry with him, or what? What do you think the father should do?*

[4] *How do you think we are like the younger son? How do you think God is like the good Father? Jesus told us this story so we would know, when we sin and do something wrong, that we can come to God and confess our sin—and know that God will forgive us.*

Jesus Listens and Helps
Luke 18:35–43

How could Jesus hear just one person in such a crowd?

Background Serious illness in the family can bring a number of problems. There may be financial difficulties. There is sure to be anxiety if the illness is serious. There are readjustments each family member must make. Probably one of the most common stresses originates in the sense of helplessness that often comes. Adults and children may feel extremely insecure and yet may not recognize this source of inner tensions. If the family life has been tightly structured, with an established and familiar routine which is now necessarily broken, the adjustments will be particularly difficult.

This familiar Bible story provides a basis for inner peace, even when the circumstances of our lives are drastically altered by illness.

194

"**W**hat's happening! What's happening!"
The blind beggar sitting by the road could hear people moving all around him. He could hear excited voices. An even larger crowd was coming. But of course the blind beggar couldn't see what it was.

"What's happening? What's happening?" the blind man asked again. No one answered him. No one paid any attention to the blind beggar at all.[1]

Probably the hardest thing for the blind beggar was that he felt so helpless. There wasn't much the blind man could do for himself.

Sometimes he felt as if no one cared about him.

Like now.

What *was* happening?

The beggar asked again, reaching out to grab at the people he could hear all around him. "What's happening?"

Finally someone told him. "Jesus. Jesus of Nazareth is walking down our road!"

No wonder everyone was so excited. Everyone in Israel knew about Jesus. Why, Jesus taught about God. And Jesus could make people well!

As soon as the blind man heard that it was Jesus coming by, he started shouting, as loudly as he could.

"Jesus!" the blind man shouted.

"Jesus, Son of David, have mercy on me! Help!"

Well, when the blind man started shouting like that, the people around shushed him.

"Be quiet!" someone said.

"Don't be so noisy," a woman said angrily.

"Yes," the whole crowd around him said. "Be quiet."

But the blind man wouldn't be quiet. He just shouted out as loud as he could. "Jesus! Help me!"

At that the crowd around the man became even angrier.

"Will you quit that noise!" the people said. "Listen," one man explained, "Jesus is much too busy and important to bother about you. You're just a blind man. You're not important at all."[2]

[1] *What do you think it would be like to be blind? What would be the worst thing about being blind? It's always hard when people are seriously ill. What has been the hardest thing for us since (name) has been sick?*

[2] *Do you suppose the blind man wasn't important enough for Jesus to bother with? Sometimes we think that God is too busy to care about our problems, or to help us. How does it make you feel inside when you aren't sure that God really cares?*

Jesus heard the blind man calling out, way at the back of the crowd. To Jesus, the blind man wasn't unimportant at all. To Jesus everyone is important.

So Jesus stopped there on the road. Jesus told some of the people to lead the blind man to Him. When the blind man came near, Jesus asked, "What do you want Me to do for you?"

We know what the blind man wanted.

He wanted to see again.

Anytime someone is ill, he wants to get well. So the blind man said to Jesus, "Lord, I want to see."

Jesus nodded His head. "Receive your sight. Your trust in Me has healed you."

And the blind man could see!

How happy the blind man was. How the blind man praised God! The crowd saw it, and they praised God too. Jesus had showed that God cares after all, and that God can help us when we trust Him.[3]

[3]*We can't know for sure when we pray that God will make us well—God may have an important reason for us to be sick. But we can know that Jesus listens and cares. God is never too busy to stop and listen to us—and care about us. Let's tell Jesus what we want, and how we feel.*

Action Idea To reinforce this sense of God's powerful presence, list with your children other illnesses about which you've prayed. Take time to praise God together for each time someone has become well.

The Widow's Gift
Mark 12:41–44

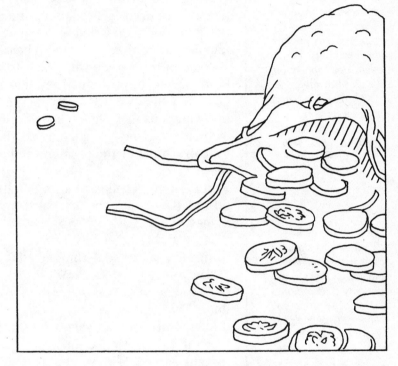

Which pile of money is worth more?

Background It takes only a few words in Mark's Gospel to describe the incident. So the incident may seem unimportant. Yet it illustrates a reality which Paul expresses in 2 Corinthians. It's not the size of the gift. It is the motivation of the giver which God values.

This story has direct application when we try to teach our children about giving, and about the use of their allowances. Even six- and seven-year-olds can sense the importance of motivation, and be glad that Jesus is happy for whatever they want to give to God.

197

[1]What are some of the
ways that the money we
give at church is used?
(If your children are
unsure, suggest a family
research project. Check
the church budget, find
pictures and locations
of missionaries,
mention study materials
children use to learn
about God, and so on.)
We give our money as
a gift to the Lord, and
it's used in many ways
to help people know
that God loves them.

Jesus and His disciples were sitting outside the great temple-church in Jerusalem. As they sat, they watched people bring offerings to God. In those days, the people brought their gifts and put them in a big wooden chest outside the temple.

The gifts they brought were used in many ways. Some money was used to provide food and clothing for the ministers and their families. Some was used to keep the temple, where they worshiped, beautiful.[1]

Some of the people who came to give money to the Lord walked in proudly. They had a lot of money to give, and they wanted everyone at the temple to see how generous they were. I imagine some of them threw in their gold and silver coins so they clinked loudly. Probably most of the people watching them were impressed.

But not everyone gave a lot of money. Some slipped up quietly to the wooden chest and put just a little money in.[2]

Jesus and His disciples watched.

And Jesus said something to His disciples.

"Do you see that woman?" Jesus said. Jesus pointed to a woman in old clothes, who looked very tired and thin. "That woman is a widow."

"Yes," the disciples said. "We see her. She didn't put much in the offering, did she?"

Jesus agreed. "No, she put in only two pennies. But those two pennies were more special to God than the thousands of dollars the rich people have just put in."

The disciples were surprised. How could two pennies be more important to God than thousands of dollars?[3]

Jesus explained. "The rich people who gave a lot have a lot left over.

"The poor widow didn't have much. She only had two pennies. But she loved God so much she gave all she had to the Lord."

God wants us to give because we love Him. It's not how much we have to give that is important to God. It's how much our gifts come from our love for Him.

[2]What do you suppose
the people watching
thought of those who
put only a little money
in? Why? What do you
suppose God thought
about them?

[3]What do you suppose
Jesus will say? How can
two pennies be more
important than
thousands of dollars?
What do you suppose
God cares most about
when we give our
offerings to Him?

198

Action Idea Don't press your children to give more, or even to set a specific amount. God's desire is for "cheerful givers," who are motivated by love to share what they have.

But do follow up on the research project of how the Lord's money is used in your church. Our giving is purposive, not a ritual obligation. We freely choose what we give, motivated by love for God and for His people.

A person in Bible times would work all day for the bigger coin, called a denarius. That coin would buy a man and his family a day's food. The tiny coin, called a "mite" in some Bibles, was only enough to buy a bit of bread and some fruit.

Faithful in Little Things
Matthew 25:14–26

Why are even children's chores important to God?

Background Boys and girls these days have few opportunities to take significant responsibility. Probably some of us parents are frustrated, trying to find some task around the house our children can do to help them build good work habits. If you've felt that frustration, the parable of the talents, told in this passage, is reassuring. In the parable we see that faithfulness in small things—the kinds of things that children can do—is a vital element in developing responsible adults. This Bible story will help you affirm their successes—and confirm their feelings that they are growing well.

This story should be told after (not before) your child has been faithful in carrying out some regular chore or responsibility. For this Bible story communicates God's, and your own, warm approval.

Once Jesus told a story to help us realize how important little things are. It's a story I'm telling you now, because I think you are like the faithful servants in Jesus' story. Here is what Jesus said:

Once a man planned to go on a long journey. So he called all his servants and gave them special responsibilities.

To one servant, he gave $5,000 to invest for him.

To the second servant, he gave $2,000 to invest for him.

To the third, he gave $1,000 to invest for him. Then the man went on his journey, and left the servants to take care of his money.

While the man was gone, the servants planned how to invest the money their master had left in their care. The servant with $5,000 started a business, and he earned $5,000 more. The servant with $2,000 started a business, and he earned $2,000 more. The servant with $1,000 was different. He hid the money and didn't use it at all!

Some time later the master of the servants came back home from his trip. Then he called his servants to him and asked what had happened to the money each had been given. How had each servant carried out his responsibilities?

The first servant came and brought his master the $5,000 he'd been given—and the $5,000 more he had earned. The master was very pleased. "Well done, good and faithful servant!" the master said. "You have been faithful with a few things; I will put you in charge of many things. Come share your master's happiness."

Now, $5,000 sounds like a lot. But the master was very rich. It was only a little to him. What the master had wanted most of all was for his servant to be faithful and carry out his responsibility.

Faithfulness in little things makes us all able to grow and be responsible for bigger things.

When the second servant came and brought his master the $2,000 he'd been given, and the $2,000 more he had earned, the master was just as pleased. The master said exactly the same thing to the servant with the $2,000 that he had said to the servant with the $5,000: "You have been faithful with a few things; I will put you in charge of many things. Come share your master's happiness."

What the master was glad about was that the servant had been faithful. The servant carried out his responsibility. The servant had grown up. He could be trusted for bigger things.

But when the third servant came, he brought only the $1,000 he had been given. He hadn't been faithful or used what the master gave him. The master was very upset with this servant. It wasn't so much the money. It was that the servant had been wicked and lazy. The servant hadn't carried out his responsibility. So the master took the $1,000 away from him and gave it to the first servant, who was responsible.

Action Idea/Talkable   *Now, why do you suppose I told you this Bible story? Can you think of any responsibilities you have had that you've faithfully carried out? They don't have to be big or important things . . . our responsibilities can seem small. What counts with God and with me is that you are faithful in doing them.*

(Explain the responsibilities you had in mind, and tell your child how happy it makes you to see him or her be faithful. You are happiest because being faithful in little things means he or she is growing up. You are happy and proud that your child is growing up and is becoming more responsible.)

Let's pray, because I want to thank God that you are like Jesus' faithful servants, growing up to be responsible.

Jesus Prays at Gethsemane
Matthew 26:36–46

What did Jesus pray the night before He was crucified?

Background Prayer is essentially simple: We come to God in trust and dependence to share, praise, and make our requests. Sometimes people try to make prayer complicated, and worry if they are "doing it right." At other times, we even hesitate to encourage our children to pray about serious needs, for fear that if God does not answer the prayer their young faith may be disturbed. When we draw back from prayer, however, we misjudge the nature of our relationship with God—or misjudge the capacity of our children to handle that reality. God is not concerned with forms or with conditions to be met. He is concerned with us. Our children can come to terms with a world in which God answers prayers according to God's understanding of what is best for us, not just our desires.

Jesus had just shared supper with His disciples. It was the last supper they would have together, and Jesus was sorrowful. He knew He would soon have to die. They ate, and talked, and they sang a hymn. Then they went outside together.

Jesus led His disciples to a place on a hillside where there was a grove of olive trees. The grove was called Gethsemane. There He told most of His disciples to rest and said, "Wait here while I pray."

When a person feels worried and upset and troubled, and is hurting inside as Jesus was, the best thing to do is to talk to God. We can ask God to help.

That's just what Jesus did. He took three disciples, Peter and James and John, and went on into the grove of trees. Jesus told His disciples how He felt. "I'm overwhelmed with sorrow, so much I feel almost ready to die," Jesus said. Then Jesus went on further and fell on the ground to pray to God the Father.[1]

[1]Have you felt worried and upset and sorrowful, as Jesus felt that night? Tell us about the time. What did you pray then, when you felt so badly? What do you think Jesus asked God the Father?

Jesus knew that soon His friends would desert Him. He knew that soon His enemies would capture and beat Him. Jesus knew that very soon He would have to die on the cross. He knew how terribly He would have to suffer. So when Jesus lay there on the ground, feeling so sorrowful, He prayed and said, "My Father, if it is possible, may this cup be taken from Me. Yet not as I will, but as You will" (Matt. 26:39).

Three times Jesus, feeling so sorrowful and upset inside, prayed this prayer to God.

In making His prayer, Jesus said three important things. First, Jesus said "My Father." Jesus knew God loved Him, and is a loving Father. Because we know God does love us we know He listens to our prayers and wants to help. Second, Jesus told God the Father what He wanted. We can always be honest with God. We can tell God what we really feel, and what we want. Jesus didn't want to have to suffer. Third, Jesus told God, "Not as I will, but as You will." Why is that important? Jesus knew that God the Father knows best. God, who loves us, will do what is best. So prayer isn't telling God what He should do. Prayer is telling God how we feel and what we want, but knowing that God will do what is best for everyone.

Jesus prayed His prayer three times, because He was so sorrowful and upset. God listened to Jesus' prayer, as a loving Father does. God did answer that prayer. He did what was best.

Jesus died on the cross and suffered for us.

But then Jesus was raised to life again.

Because Jesus died for us, and came to life, our sins can be forgiven. One day you and I will be with the Lord forever because Jesus suffered so for us. After the suffering was over, Jesus was glad that He had asked God to do what the Father knew was best.[2]

Action Idea Talk about prayers that have been answered. If you keep an "I prayed, God answered" book look over the list and see how many times God has said yes to your prayers. Talk too about the "No" answers. Can you see now the good that God intended for you by saying no? We can't always see the good. But because we trust God, we know that He will only give us what is best.

[2]*Do you suppose we can pray as Jesus did? How? (Help your children see the three elements: come to God as Father, express feelings and requests, ask God to do what is best.) Many, many times God gives us just what we ask for. But sometimes God says no, and we don't get what we asked for. But because we know God loves us, we know that what God does give us may hurt for a time, but will really bring us something that is good.*

Jesus Is Arrested
Matthew 26:47–56

Why would people want to hurt Jesus?

Background This is one of a sequence of three Easter stories. The Easter season is one of the two great highlights of the Christian year. Like Christmas, it marks an event which makes our Christian faith unique.

These three stories do not feature *talkables* within the story. Instead the *Action Ideas* suggest ways to create a context in the home which will help our children appreciate Easter events and enter into both the sufferings and the exaltation of our Lord.

The stories are retold for the whole family. They can be read or told as a family tradition, repeated each year. Used this way they will take on deeper meaning each year, as our children grow older and are better able to understand.

206

"This is the last supper we will have together," Jesus told His disciples.

A few minutes before disciples had been happy. They were eating supper with Jesus.

But then Jesus told His disciples He would soon leave them, to go to God the Father. Jesus told them to love each other while He was away.

Jesus didn't tell His disciples the terrible things that were about to happen to Him. But Jesus knew.

One of the things that Jesus knew was this: one of His own disciples was going to betray Him. So Jesus said it. "I tell you the truth, one of you will betray Me."

Most of Jesus' disciples were shocked. "Is it I, Lord?" they asked. "Surely I won't be the one to betray You."

When the disciple named Judas asked the question, Jesus dipped some bread in wine and gave it to him. "You are the one," Jesus told Judas.

Right away Judas got up and went out of the room. Judas went to the chief priests, who were Jesus' enemies. The chief priests had already decided to kill Jesus. They didn't like Jesus to teach about God. And they didn't want Jesus to do miracles.

Judas and the chief priests talked and then made an agreement. "All right," Judas said. "You pay me thirty pieces of silver money, and I'll show you where you can take Jesus prisoner."

Jesus and His disciples walked down in the valley and up the side of the hill on the other side—a hill called the Mount of Olives. There Jesus found a grove of olive trees, called Gethsemane. Jesus stopped to pray. Jesus prayed alone, because His disciples were tired and had gone to sleep.

Jesus knew what was going to happen. He knew how much He would suffer soon. And Jesus wept as He talked with His heavenly Father.

Now Judas led the mob of Jesus' enemies up the side of the Mount of Olives. Judas knew where Jesus would go. Jesus usually stopped and rested there when He left Jerusalem.

Jesus knew that Judas was coming.

He woke up His sleeping disciples.

He was ready to be arrested, and to suffer, and to die.

When Judas came up to Jesus and the others, he went right up to the Lord. Judas gave Jesus a kiss and said, "Greetings!" That kiss was a signal. Judas had agreed to betray Jesus, and to point Jesus out to the high priest's guards. "The one I kiss will be the one you want," Judas had told them.

Only one of Jesus' friends tried to help. Peter grabbed a sword and swung it wildly at one of the high priest's servants.

"Put your sword away," Jesus said. "Don't you know that I can call on God the Father, and God will send armies of angels to help Me? But what the Bible says must happen has to happen."

Jesus must die for our sins. He must rise to life again. This must happen, even though death for Jesus meant terrible suffering.

As the mob roughly dragged Jesus down the hill, all Jesus' followers ran away in fright. Jesus was alone.

In the next hours Jesus would experience much suffering—and then He would die.

(Pray together, thanking Jesus for being willing to suffer for us.)

Action Idea　Symbols can help to make this time special for children and for adults. See if you and your family can work out a symbol to help you remember Jesus' suffering this Easter time. It might be something as simple as a teardrop, drawn on a 3x5 card. It might be something more complicated, such as a large circle divided into sections, each of which has a picture representing some Easter event (such as a crown of thorns, a cross, and so on).

Begin your Easter remembrance on Good Friday eve. Read this first story in the Easter sequence. Then together work out your family Easter symbol for this year.

Peter Denies Jesus
Matthew 26:69–79

What would make Peter lie about being Jesus' friend?

Background Two common childhood themes are picked up and amplified in this familiar Bible story. Boys and girls, particularly as they move through early childhood into ages nine and eleven, feel great pressure to conform to their peers. Children of all ages find it as easy, as do adults, to shade the truth, or to tell outright lies to avoid unpleasantness. Certainly the apostle Peter must have been able to understand those pressures. The night of Jesus' arrest and trial, Peter surrendered to peer pressure and lied about his relationship with the Lord.

"You're one of His followers!"

It was just a servant girl who said it, but Peter looked around, frightened.

"Yes, you are," the girl said. "You were with Jesus in Galilee."

Peter didn't know what to do.

That night Jesus had been arrested. Jesus was inside the house of the high priest, being tried by His enemies. Peter had followed the gang of guards who captured Jesus. Now Peter was sitting in the courtyard outside the house of the high priest, worrying about what was going to happen to Jesus.

Peter thought he was safe. Peter thought no one knew him. But then the servant girl said, out loud, right in front of all the others outside the house that night, "You are one of Jesus' followers."

Peter looked around. Everyone was looking at him. Peter knew that none of those people liked Jesus. He was afraid if he told them he really was one of Jesus' followers, the people in the courtyard might hurt him. So Peter did a terrible thing. He lied and said in front of everyone, "I don't know what you're talking about."[1]

[1]Have you ever felt that everyone was looking at you, wanting you to do something you didn't think you should? Can you tell us about it?

Peter must have been very ashamed of himself for lying about his friendship with Jesus. But Peter had been afraid of the other people. Now he hunched back in the shadows. When it seemed people were still looking at him, Peter got up and went outside the gate.

There another servant girl saw him. She pointed at Peter and told the people who were waiting outside the gate, "This fellow was with Jesus of Nazareth."

Now Peter had a chance to do the right thing! People were still looking at Peter. People who didn't like Jesus were watching. And the girl said it again. "This fellow was with Jesus."[2]

[2]What do you suppose Peter feels now? What do you think Peter will do? Will it be hard or easy for Peter to admit he is one of Jesus' friends?

Peter looked around at the people who were watching him. He was still afraid. Before he knew it, Peter spoke up and said roughly, "I don't know the man. I swear it, I don't even know this Jesus."

Peter lied again!

Peter had been afraid of what others would think and do to him, and Peter had lied.[3]

Peter felt really ashamed now. But before Peter could slip away, several men in the group came up to Peter. "We think you are one of the followers of Jesus. You talk with a Galilean accent, and Jesus is from there. The way you talk gives you away."

This was the third time now that people were staring at Peter. Peter looked around. He was still afraid. Peter worried more about what other people would think of him than about what Jesus would think of him. For the third time, Peter lied about his friendship for Jesus.

As soon as the words came out of Peter's mouth, a rooster crowed nearby. Then Peter remembered something Jesus had said. Just that night, before Jesus was taken prisoner, Jesus told Peter, "You will deny Me three times before the cock crows to announce the morning."

Now Peter felt sorry and was very ashamed. As Peter left the yard of the high priest's house, he wept bitterly.[4]

Let's ask God to help us make choices that please the Lord.

Action Idea   To remind the children to make right choices, make a small "rooster" symbol. It can be attached to school books or playthings as a reminder to please Jesus instead of friends, when friends want us to do something that is wrong.

[3]*Do you suppose it's more important to do what our friends want, or what's right? What do you think could help people in situations like Peter's to do right?*

[4]*Have you ever felt like Peter did, guilty and ashamed and sorry after you'd done something wrong? How much better it would be if Peter—and you and I—could remember to do what pleases God.*

Jesus Is Crucified
Luke 23; John 19

Why did Jesus die on the cross?

Background This is the second in a series of three stories retold especially for family Easter observance. The first story is found on page 206 and the third is on page 217.

In our family, we found that it helped make Easter and Christmas special to hold private family services later at night, after our chil-dren's usual bedtimes. Getting to stay up late was exciting to the children—and one way to underline the specialness of the occasion. Nighttime candlelight services, with the family gathered close together to share the wonder and glory of Jesus' self-giving, can enrich the faith of each individual in your home.

"**H**it Him!" one of the leaders shouted.

"Yes, hit Him!" And the men began to hit Jesus and spit on Him.

For hours the enemies of Jesus had tried to get witnesses to lie about Jesus, so their court could condemn Him. Finally the high priest asked Jesus: "Tell us the truth. Are You the Christ, the Son of God?"

Jesus answered them honestly.

After all, Jesus had told everyone so many times. "Yes," Jesus said, "it is as you say. And in the future you will see Me, the Son of Man, sitting at the right hand of God the Father, coming on the clouds of heaven."

It was then the leaders shouted, "Hit Him."

Jesus had claimed He was the Son of God.

Because the leaders didn't believe Jesus, they thought what Jesus said was a great crime. "He deserves to die," the leaders said. In their anger, they slapped Jesus and hit Him with their fists.

But the high priest and the leaders of the Jewish court had a problem. Israel was governed by Rome. It was part of the Roman Empire. The Jewish court didn't have power to put anyone to death.

So after they had beaten Jesus, the leaders took Jesus to Pilate, the Roman governor. They told the Roman governor that Jesus was a criminal and ought to be killed. "Why," the leaders said, "this Jesus says He is our King."

When the Roman governor heard their charges he wanted to talk with Jesus. "Are you really King of the Jews?" Pilate asked.

Jesus answered Pilate. "Yes. But My kingdom is a heavenly kingdom, and My followers don't fight."

After Pilate talked with Jesus, he knew that Jesus was innocent. The Roman governor realized that the chief priests and religious leaders were just jealous of Jesus. So Pilate wanted to let Jesus go.

Pilate called all Jesus' enemies back into the courtroom.

"I know this Man is innocent," Pilate said.

But the enemies of Jesus shouted and screamed. "Crucify Him! Crucify Him!"

Pilate didn't want to have Jesus put to death. So he tried something else. Every year at the time of the Passover Feast, the Roman governor released a Jewish prisoner as a special favor. The governor let the people of Israel choose who should be released.

So Pilate had an idea. "Should I release Jesus for you, or should I release Barabbas?"

Barabbas was a brutal criminal who had robbed and killed. Jesus was a good man. He taught about God and healed the sick. Pilate thought for sure that the crowd would want Jesus released rather than the evil Barabbas.

But Jesus' enemies had stirred up the crowd against Jesus. When the Roman governor asked the crowd to choose, Jesus' enemies began to shout. "We want Barabbas!" "Turn Barabbas loose!"

Pilate was surprised.

"What about Jesus?" Pilate asked.

"Kill Him!" the crowd shouted. "Crucify Jesus! Yes, crucify Jesus!"

Pilate didn't want to crucify Jesus. He knew Jesus was innocent. But Pilate was afraid. Pilate, the Roman governor of Jerusalem, was afraid that the Jewish leaders who hated Jesus would go to Rome, and say that Pilate let someone go who claimed to be a king. So Pilate gave in.

"It is your responsibility," Pilate said to the crowd. And then Pilate gave the order.

Jesus was to be crucified.

The first thing that happened, the Roman soldiers took Jesus to a nearby guardroom. There the soldiers beat Jesus with whips. This was to make Jesus bleed, to make Him weak from loss of blood. Jesus would die quicker if He was weak.

The soldiers also put a crown made out of sharp thorns on Jesus' head. Then the soldiers beat Jesus some more. They spit on Him and made fun of Him.

Jesus just stood there, quietly accepting the suffering.

Finally it was time for the execution.

The soldiers took Jesus outside and tried to make Him carry the long wooden pole used to make the cross. Jesus staggered under the heavy weight. He stumbled along the stone streets. Finally Jesus fell under the weight of the cross.

The soldiers grabbed an onlooker and made him carry the cross. Jesus, weak from loss of blood, staggered on through the city streets after them.

Finally they all came to the city gates.

Just outside the gates was a hill, a hill that looked like a skull. In Hebrew its name was Golgotha. We usually call the hill Calvary.

The soldiers took Jesus' clothes and then threw Him down on the ground. They nailed Jesus' hands and feet to the wooden cross. Then they lifted the cross up and stood it upright in a hole that had been dug.

Jesus was hanging on the cross.

He was about to die—for our sins.

While Jesus hung on the cross, wonderful things happened. Even though it was about noon, the sky suddenly became very dark. The whole land was covered with darkness, as if it were night. The watching soldiers were amazed. They began to realize that Jesus was special after all.

Jesus wasn't crucified alone.

Two thieves were crucified at the same time. At first the two ridiculed Jesus. They said, "If You're really God's Son, come down from the cross." All the crowd watching the crucifixion jeered and said the same things.

They didn't know that Jesus was dying for our sins.

Later one of the two thieves changed his mind. "Don't you know," that thief said to the other, "that we are dying for our crimes? Jesus hasn't done anything wrong." And the dying thief said to Jesus, "Remember me when You come into Your kingdom." Jesus promised, "Today you will be with Me in Paradise [heaven]."

The thief who believed in Jesus was forgiven.

Jesus was dying to pay for the thief's sins, and for our sins, too.

Jesus suffered on the cross for a long time.

It wasn't just the pain, even though crucifixion hurts terribly. What made Jesus suffer most was the weight of sins that He carried there—the sins of the whole world. For the very first time, God the Father had to turn away from God the Son. Jesus took on Himself all of our sins. He died for the wickedness that human beings have done.

Then it was time.

Jesus looked up to heaven and dismissed His spirit. His suffering was over, and Jesus died.

Jesus didn't have to die.

Jesus was God, and He could have come down from the cross. Jesus could have destroyed all His enemies. But Jesus chose to die, because Jesus knew that your sins and mine must be paid for. Jesus wanted to forgive us, so we could become members of God's family.

Jesus suffered.

But Jesus was glad to suffer.

Jesus suffered for you and for me.

Action Idea Conclude the reading of this solemn account of the Crucifixion with a family communion. You can read the service from 1 Corinthians 11:23–26, or write your own communion service. As your children grow, your communion service can be expanded, modified, or rewritten yearly in preparation for the special family time when you remember together Jesus' death.

Jesus Is Risen!
Matthew 28; John 21

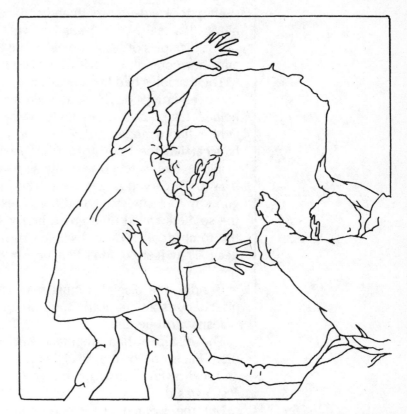

Where could Jesus' body be?

Background Jesus' resurrection stands in history as glowing, final proof of all our Lord's claims about Himself. Easter reveals Jesus as the triumphant Son of God. Easter reveals all the divine power and the glory that were masked during our Savior's years on earth.

The Russian church greets Easter morning with a symbolic search, followed by glad cries of "He is risen! He is risen indeed!"

Because Easter is so special, we will want to share its joy in our family. This Bible story is suggested for use early Easter morning, to set the tone for the day's joyful celebration at worship. This is the third in a series of three stories for use during the Easter season. The first two stories are found on pages 206 and 212.

217

"He's alive!"

The women were almost out of breath when they ran into the home where Jesus' disciples were mourning.

Mary took a deep breath and choked out the exciting news: "It's really true. Jesus is alive!"

The disciples of Jesus looked at the excited women— and they couldn't believe what they heard!

The disciples had been heartbroken ever since Jesus had been crucified. They had seen Jesus die. Some had helped take Jesus' dead body down from the cross. Others had wrapped Jesus' body in linen cloths. They had carried the body to a nearby garden. There the disciples had watched tearfully as Jesus' body was put in a tomb carved in the rock. The disciples had said good-by to Jesus. They had loved Jesus so much. But the soldiers rolled up a great, heavy stone and closed the tomb door. So the disciples knew that Jesus was dead. They just couldn't believe what the woman told them.

Besides, the disciples must have thought, the chief priests put soldiers at the tomb to guard the door.

Jesus *must* be dead.

The disciples had wept and sorrowed after Jesus died. Each one of the disciples knew he would weep and feel awful sorrow for the rest of his life because Jesus was dead.

But the women knew better. Loudly, the women shouted out their story to the sorrowful disciples.

"Listen," one of them probably said. She told the disciples how they went to the tomb early in the morning, with flowers and with spices for Jesus' dead body. But when the women got to the tomb, the guards were gone and the stone was rolled away. Jesus' tomb was open. An angel, as bright as the brightest lightning, sat on the stone that had locked Jesus' body in.

The woman told the disciples how the angel had talked with them. "Don't be afraid," the angel said. "Jesus, who was crucified, isn't here. Jesus has come to life again, just as He said He would. Jesus is risen from the dead."

The angel then told the women to go look inside the tomb. The women looked. The angel was right! Jesus wasn't there at all. Jesus had come back from the dead!

Then the angel sent the women to the disciples. "Go quickly," the angel said, "and tell His disciples that Jesus has risen from the dead and is going to Galilee." The angel promised that the disciples would see Jesus there.

The women started to run.

They ran as fast as they could.

Suddenly, there in front of the hurrying women, was Jesus Himself! The women actually saw Jesus! Full of joy they fell at Jesus' feet and worshiped Him. Now the women knew for sure. Their friend Jesus, the one whom they loved so much, really was the Son of God.

When the women reached the disciples, all out of breath, they shouted out the good news.

"Jesus is alive!"

"He lives. We saw Him ourselves."

When Jesus' disciples heard the story, they began to wonder. Could it be true?

Two other disciples were beginning to believe too. Peter and John had not been with the rest. Even earlier that morning, Mary Magdalene had visited the garden tomb. Mary Magdalene thought someone had stolen the body, so Mary came, crying, to tell Peter and John.

Peter began to run toward the tomb. John followed. Because John was younger he outran Peter. When John and Peter reached the tomb, each looked inside. There were the strips of linen cloth Jesus had been wrapped in. But Jesus wasn't there! How could the linen be there, and Jesus be gone?

Peter and John looked. And they began to believe. Jesus really had risen from the dead!

That night all the disciples met together in a private room. The door was locked, and the disciples were talking. What had happened? Was Jesus really alive again?

And suddenly, there was Jesus.

Alive.

Right there in the room with the disciples!

"Peace," Jesus said to His amazed disciples. Then Jesus showed them His hands, where the spikes were driven when He was nailed to the cross. Jesus showed them His side, and they saw the wound made by a Roman soldier's spear.

It really was Jesus!

There could be no mistake.

Jesus was alive again.

And the disciples were filled with joy.

Jesus *is* alive. Today. Because Jesus lives, we will live too, forever and forever with God.

> **Action Idea** Early Easter morning, why not imitate the Russian Church's practice? Get up at dawn. Search through your whole house, and outside too. Jesus' body is not there. He is risen.
>
> Greet each other with the words of joy:
>
> "Jesus is risen. Jesus is risen indeed."
>
> Then fill your home with joyful Easter music until you go together to church, to celebrate, with other believers, the resurrection of our Lord.

Jesus Trusts Peter

John 21:15–19

Why would Peter want to hide from Jesus?

Background This beautiful Bible story helps our children and us understand the transforming power of forgiveness. When God forgives us, He breaks the bonds forged by our past failures. God tells us to look ahead. Looking ahead, we realize that God intends to help us grow to spiritual maturity. God intends to use us and to make us spiritually significant persons.

Children of any age who feel discouraged about their failures will sense God's love and His belief in them as you share this Bible story of Jesus' conversation with Peter after Peter had denied Jesus three times.

Jesus stood up.

Jesus had been crouched over a fire, cooking some bread and fish for His disciples. The disciples had gone fishing. But when a Man on shore called them and then brought them food, the disciples knew it was Jesus.

Peter stood behind some of the other disciples, keeping them between him and Jesus. Peter did this because he was ashamed. He was afraid of what Jesus might say to him.

You see, just before Jesus was crucified and raised again from the dead, Peter had done a terrible thing. Peter had been so afraid of what people might think that Peter lied three times about his friendship for Jesus.

Now Peter remembered how terribly he had failed. So Peter didn't want Jesus to see him. Peter just wanted to hide.[1]

Peter felt very ashamed. Peter felt as if he was no good at all. He had failed Jesus and had failed himself too. Now Peter was afraid that Jesus would never trust him again.

But Jesus didn't let Peter hide.

When they finished eating, Jesus looked right at Peter. "Peter," Jesus asked, "do you truly love Me more than these?"

Peter nodded. "Yes, Lord. You know that I love You."

Then Jesus said, "Peter, take care of My sheep."

Jesus asked Peter again, "Do you love Me?"

Peter gave the same answer. "Yes, Lord, You know that I love You." Then Jesus said, "Peter, take care of My sheep."

Peter had denied Jesus three times. So Jesus asked Peter His question a third time. "Peter, do you love Me?"

Peter felt hurt that Jesus questioned him a third time. "Yes, Lord," Peter said, "You know all things. You know that I love You."

Then Jesus said to Peter, "Feed My sheep."

We knows that Jesus' "sheep" are people who love

[1]What words do you suppose might describe how Peter felt then? Have you ever failed and just didn't want others to see you? Can you tell us about one time?

222

God and believe in Him. What Jesus did was to give Peter a special job. Peter was going to be a leader and a teacher, to love and care for the people whom Jesus loves.[2]

Jesus knew how badly Peter had failed. But Jesus knew that Peter really did love Him. Jesus knew that Peter, even though he had failed, would become a good leader for God's people. He trusted Peter enough to give Peter an important job. Jesus knew that Peter would grow and change. Jesus knew that God would help Peter become a good leader in spite of his failures.[3]

> *Action Idea*   Make a poster for your child's room on an "I'm Growing" theme. You can use any of a number of possible motifs to represent growth. Trace a caterpillar from cocoon to a butterfly. Trace a seed from sprout to plant to flower. You can also include a helpful saying, such as, "I don't give up. God isn't finished with me yet."
>
> Work together to design and make each child's own unique "growing" poster. How good to know that you truly can believe in your child, whatever his failures, because God *isn't* finished with him yet. God is at work. Jesus in our lives brings solid hope for the future.

[2]*Do you think Peter was a good choice for this important job? Why—or why not? Why do you suppose that Jesus would trust someone who had failed him so badly?*

[3]*Everyone has times when they fail and fail. When that happens to you, I don't give up on you. I know that you will keep on growing. I know that God will help you grow, as He helped Peter. God will help you be able to succeed.*

Jesus Returns to Heaven
John 14:1–4; Acts 1:1–11

What would you have thought if you watched Jesus return to heaven?

Background Death and dying are facts of life, even for children. Few experiences are likely to cause more grief than the loss of a beloved family member. Few experiences are likely to create more doubts and concerns about a child's personal future.

Several Bible stories in this book are related to death. Each focuses on some specific childhood concern. The story of the death of Moses is designed to help a child deal with the death of a grandparent or other older person. The story of Stephen deals with sudden, unexpected death. This Bible story explains what happens when a believer dies, and it recalls Jesus' own words about what He is now doing in heaven to prepare a place for us.

224

It was time to leave.

Jesus took one last walk with His disciples.

How excited the disciples had been when they learned that Jesus was alive. When Jesus was crucified, and died, all that the disciples felt were sorrow and grief. How lonely the disciples had felt then. It seemed to them that they were empty inside. Jesus was dead, and the disciples thought they would never see Jesus again.[1]

It was hard for the disciples when their friend Jesus died. But how excited and joyful they felt on Easter morning, when they discovered that Jesus was alive again! Death hadn't been the end for Jesus. Jesus came back from the dead, to be with His friends.

But Jesus wasn't going to stay with the disciples. That's why the walk Jesus and His friends took one morning was their last walk. Jesus was going to leave them. The disciples knew that Jesus was alive. But Jesus would soon be gone, as if He'd taken a long trip.

(If you've gone on a long trip, or your family members live at a distance, talk about this as analogous to dying. We are not with our distant loved ones every day. But we know they are all right. We may miss them. But we don't feel sad, as though we would never see them again.)

"Don't let your hearts be troubled," Jesus had said. "Trust in God; trust also in Me. There are many rooms in My Father's house. I am going there—to be with God the Father. When I go I will prepare a place for you."

Jesus was going to heaven to be with God the Father. Jesus would have heaven ready for you and me. Jesus wanted the disciples to know that when they died, there was a special place all ready for them with God. Dying is like taking a long trip for us too. We go to be with Jesus, in a wonderful place Jesus is preparing for us.[2]

Jesus made another wonderful promise to His disciples. Jesus told them that He would prepare a place for them. And Jesus told them, "I will come back, and take you to be with Me, that you also may be where I am."

[1] *How do you suppose the disciples who loved Jesus felt when He died? Why is it so hard for us when someone we love dies?*

[2] *How do you suppose the disciples felt when Jesus told them about heaven? What made them most happy? To know that when their bodies died they would go on living? To know that when they died they would be in a beautiful place prepared just for them? Or to know that when they died they would be with Jesus always? Or perhaps to know that the people they loved who had died were still alive in heaven, so some day they would be together again? Which of these seems most important to you when you think about dying?*

Jesus would leave. But He will come back again.

Then all of us—people who are alive then, and people who have died—will be together again. Then we will all be together, with Jesus, forever.

Jesus did return to heaven. While His friends watched, He rose up the air and finally disappeared. When Jesus was gone, and the amazed disciples were still looking up, two angels stood beside them.

"Men of Galilee," the angels said. "Why do you stand here, looking into the sky? This same Jesus, who has been taken from you into heaven, will come back in the same way you have seen Him go into heaven."

Then the disciples knew for sure. Jesus was gone, and they wouldn't see Him again here on earth. But when the disciples died, they would go to heaven, and Jesus would be there. Someday, perhaps soon, Jesus will come back again. Then we will all be together in heaven, forever and ever.

Action Idea The sense that people who die are not just gone and forgotten is important to children. You can help by talking about loved ones who have died, whom you are looking forward to being with when Jesus comes again. Tell stories about your own parents (if they have died) or about grandparents or friends you knew as a child. Speak of them with warmth and humor and gladness, as though they were still living (for they are). Your own confidence in the promise Jesus made will go far to build your child's faith and hope.

TALKABLE STORIES FROM THE REST OF THE NEW TESTAMENT

The New Church Lives in Love

Acts 2:44–47

Why would Jedediah give his lunch to a friend?

Background The people of Jerusalem looked with amazement at the new community that formed after Jesus' resurrection and said of the Christians, "See how they love each other!" That new community, marked by sharing and love, is described in many New Testament passages. We read of its life-style in nearly every epistle, and gradually grasp the importance of the acceptance, forgiveness, mutual support and encouragement which made the early Body of Christ such a dynamic witness. These people truly cared about each other. That caring, in a world in which people are hungry for love, is a warm call to come to Jesus and so become one of Jesus' people.

It was so exciting. To have real friends at last! That's what Jedediah was thinking as he hurried to the home of his neighbor, Jeremy.

Jedediah was a Christian in the very first church, a church started in Jerusalem after Jesus' resurrection. Jedediah and Jeremy are made-up names. But the Bible tells us the kind of things that happened to them as they learned how to live together in love.

One of the things that made Jedediah so happy about his new Christian friends was that people were so unselfish. When Jeremy's family ran out of money, because Jeremy was hurt and couldn't work, other Christians brought food and money to help them. Jedediah didn't have much, but he brought some food for the family too. Jedediah had to skip his own lunch. But it made him very happy to be able to help others. *Yes,* Jedediah thought, *being one of Jesus' people made one feel very happy. Joyful even.*

It was also fun to be together. The new friends got together almost every day. They ate at each other's homes and liked to be with each other. These were friends a person could talk to. You could talk to these new friends about your problems, or tell them if you felt upset. These friends really cared. Why, they even prayed for each other. They talked to God about what was important to each other.

For Jedediah, real friends were special. These friends of his had many things in common. They believed in Jesus as their Savior. They all tried to please the Lord. Oh, Jedediah had friends who weren't Christians, of course. But his closest friends were people like him, who tried to please the Lord because they loved Jesus. Worshiping God together, and knowing that your friends would want to do what is right, was good. These friends wouldn't try to get you to do something wrong. That was one of the things that made the new church so warm and wonderful.

When Jedediah was with his Christian friends, Jedediah knew he belonged. He was with people whom he was learning to love. Jedediah knew that these friends would love him, too, always.

Oh look! There is Jeremy now.

"Hi Jeremy!" Jedediah shouted. He hurried toward Jeremy. Jedediah was with his friends.

Talkables Rather than weaving the talkables in, here are a number of ideas for following up on themes introduced in the story. You may want to talk about all or just some of these areas.

1. How did people like Jedediah, in the first church, show they loved each other? (List from the story, or read it through again to make a complete list.) Which way of showing love do you think was most important? Can you think of other ways friends act, that show they care about each other?

2. Who are your closest friends? Jedediah's closest friends were Christians who wanted to please God, as he did. Why might it be important to have close friends who want to do what's right?

3. How can our family be like the first church, and love each other better? Are there things that any of us do that make you feel unloved? Can you tell us about them? How can we show more love to each other?

Action Idea If you apply this story to your family, work together on a mural or collage which will express ways to live with each other in love. You can use drawings, cut out the pictures and words, and so on. The finished product will remind you of how to better love each other at home, and experience the joy that comes when we really care.

The Believers Pray
Acts 4

What would you pray after you had been whipped for talking about Jesus?

Background When the disciples proclaimed the resurrected Jesus, and their message was authenticated by miracles, the religious leaders who plotted to have the Lord crucified were stunned. The death of Jesus hadn't stamped out the movement after all!

Immediately the leaders attempted to put pressure on the disciples. The leaders threatened them and warned them to stop preaching in the name of Jesus. Under this threat, the disciples gathered together. The early church went to God in prayer.

In their prayers they did not beg God to change the difficult situation. Instead the apostles accepted responsibility for facing the difficulties and asked only for God's help and empowering, that they might do what is right.

232

"**B**ring them in here," the officer said harshly.

The guards dragged Peter and John into the courtroom. Now Peter and John stood in front of the very men who had condemned Jesus to die just a few weeks before.

The judges in that courtroom were very angry. The judges had killed Jesus because they didn't like what Jesus taught, and they didn't believe that Jesus is the Son of God. Now Jesus' followers were preaching all over the city. Jesus' disciples were saying that Jesus really was God's Son. Even worse, some of the disciples of Jesus had healed people. Then they claimed that Jesus' power was what performed the miracles. The judges were sure they had to hush up people like Peter and John. If they didn't, pretty soon everyone in the city would blame the judges for killing the Lord.

That day in court, the judges angrily asked Peter and John how they had healed a crippled man.

Boldly, Peter spoke up. "We healed the crippled man by the power of Jesus Christ of Nazareth, whom you crucified, but God raised from the dead. You rejected Jesus, but I tell you that Jesus is the only way a person can be saved."

The judges sent Peter and John out of the room, and talked it over. Everyone in the city of Jerusalem knew the man had been healed. So the judges were afraid to punish Peter and John. Instead, the judges called Peter and John back, and threatened them.

"Don't you dare speak or teach in the name of Jesus," the judges said. "We have the power to punish you. If you do talk about Jesus, we'll make you suffer!"

Right away Peter and John went to join other Christians. Peter and John told about the judges' threats and warnings. The Christians began to pray.[1]

First, Peter and John told God they knew that only He is truly powerful. "Sovereign Lord," they said, "You made the earth and the seas and the heaven, and everything in them." Peter and John knew the judges who threatened them really didn't have any power at all.

[1] *What do you suppose the disciples and the Christians prayed? If you had been there, what do you think you would have wanted God to do?*

Have you ever had a time when you were afraid or worried, about what might happen if you did the right thing? If you had prayed then, what do you think you would have asked God for?

God is in charge of our lives. God can protect us. Only when God lets it happen for a good reason can anything bad happen to us.

Second, Peter and John asked God for help.

"Lord, consider their threats, and enable Your servants to speak Your Word with great boldness." Peter and John only wanted God to help them be strong inside, so they would do the right thing in spite of the threats.

Praying doesn't always change things outside. Sometimes praying is to change us inside, to make us strong so that we can do something that is hard for us.[2]

[2] Why do you suppose Peter and John prayed that kind of prayer? Do you think they wanted their difficulties to go away? Or did they think it was better to have difficulties? Why?

God did answer Peter and John's prayer. The Bible says that God the Holy Spirit gave Peter and John the strength they needed inside, so Peter and John did speak boldly about Jesus. God answered their prayer for strength inside. That was even better than if God had made the enemies go away.

Let's pray together that God will give us strength inside us, as God gave strength to Peter and John. God will help us do what we believe is right, too.

> ***Action Idea*** Make it a practice for the next few weeks when you pray together to pray for strength inside. If you are careful to continue this pattern, you can build into your children's lives a wonderful prayer experience. You can help them develop a confidence which comes only when we know God is with us, to help us do what is right.

The Believers Share

Acts 4:32–37

Why would Jedediah's mom pawn the living room rug?

Background Old and New Testaments both affirm the rights of the individual to have personal possessions. But both Testaments also enjoin generosity. What we have is ours. But when we love others, and are sensitive to their needs, we will be quick to respond by sharing.

It is striking that the term used in the New Testament to express giving is "fellowship"—a word which renders the Greek word *koinonia*, and which means "sharing." God gives us the privilege of so sharing the joys and sorrows of others that we become sensitive to their needs, and motivated by love to reach out and help.

"Zachari looks pretty upset these days," Jedediah said to some of his Christian friends.

Zachari and Jedediah aren't mentioned in the Bible. But what happened to them is the kind of thing that the Bible book of Acts tells us about. When Jesus had died and come to life again, the people who believed in Him got together often. Jesus' followers talked about the teachings of the leaders who wrote our New Testament. And Jesus' followers learned to love each other very much. They were the closest of friends.

That's why Jedediah was concerned when he noticed that Zachari seemed upset. Friends care about each other. If one friend is worried or upset, other friends want to help.[1]

Jedediah showed he was a friend by noticing that Zachari was upset. Jedediah noticed Zachari didn't smile as much as he used to. Zachari looked sad. Or Zachari stood off alone to one side when others were talking. When we see a person do those things, we can be pretty sure that something is wrong.

When times really got hard in Jerusalem, and many people had no way to earn money for food, some of the Christians sold land or houses. The Christians brought the money from the sale to the disciples. The disciples, like Peter and John, gave away the money and saw that no one would go hungry. Because Jesus' people really did love each other, they were ready to share.

God doesn't ask us to sell everything and give it away. But God does want us to be sensitive. When our friends are feeling badly, God wants us to help. Sometimes we may need to give others money to help them out. But sometimes we can help just by listening to them. Or we can help by working with a friend on a hard schoolwork assignment. We can help by having others over to play with us when they're lonely. One wonderful way to show our love to God is to love others, and help them when they need us to care.

Action Idea Make a list with your children of times when their friends or they might feel upset or unhappy

[1] *Who are the friends whom you care about the most? Do they care about you, too? How do you suppose we know when our friends really care about us? What are some things about (name of a friend identified by your child) that helps you feel he is a real friend?*

or lonely. When the list is as long as you and your children can make it, write each problem area on a separate 8½ × 11 sheet of paper.

Draw a vertical line dividing the paper into two sections. On one side of the paper, try to list with your child as many clues as possible that might indicate a friend is having problems. Listing things that your children can observe from the behavior of others will help them become sensitive to others' feelings.

On the other side of each paper, list possible ways you and your children might be able to help a person with a particular problem. A lonely child might be invited to stay overnight, and so on. You might tell a worried boy or girl you will pray for him or her, tell your parents about the problem and see if they can help, and so on.

As you work through this process together you can help your children grow significantly in their ability to relate well to others. You can also help them develop the Christian grace of caring love.

Learning to Be Fair
Acts 6:1–7

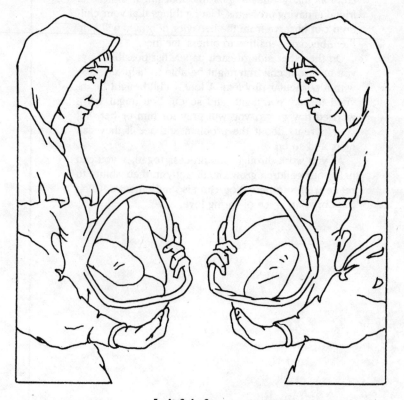

Is it fair for one person to get one loaf of bread and another five?

Background The early New Testament church was vital and loving. But it was not without problems. In a way, that church was much like a good home. The members of a family do love each other. But things happen which lead to disputes, to hurt, and even to anger. The dispute over fairness that caused bitterness in the early church is like many disputes over fairness that take place in every home. What our children need, and receive in this Bible story, is a way to work through disputes: a way that shows love and is fair to all.

"It isn't fair!"

"They're cheating us."

"How come they get more than we do?"

All these things were being said in the first church in Jerusalem. People were upset and angry. Some of the people were very jealous too.

"It isn't fair for them to get more than we do!"[1]

The people who were part of that first Jerusalem church had one special difference between them. Some of those Christians had grown up speaking the Greek language, and some had grown up speaking the language of Palestine, called Aramaic. When these people became Christians, they became part of God's one family. But they still had their differences.

What happened was that the widows and orphans, who had no one to help them earn money for food, were given food by their Christian friends. But the Christians who spoke Greek thought their Greek-speaking widows weren't getting their fair share. They were sure the Aramaic speaking widows were getting more. That's why they were upset and angry.[2]

The people in the Jerusalem church were part of God's family. They loved Jesus, and they loved each other. Being upset wasn't something the Jerusalem Christians liked. But they were hurt when they felt others didn't treat them fairly.

So the Greek-speaking Christians complained. Instead of keeping their feelings bottled up inside, or trying to hurt their Aramaic-speaking brothers, they told how they were feeling. Then Jesus' disciples, who were the leaders, called everyone together to talk about the problem.

The disciples listened to the people who felt upset and hurt. Jesus' disciples didn't blame anyone. Instead, the disciples told everyone, Aramaic and Greek-speaking alike, "You choose seven good men, who love God and who are wise, and we will make them responsible for giving out the food. They will take responsibility, and see that everyone is treated fairly."

[1] Have you ever felt the way those people felt? When are you most likely to feel upset and angry because you feel someone isn't fair?

[2] Do you think the Aramaic-speaking Christians were right to feel upset?

239

My, what a good idea, everyone thought. And all the Christians worked together to choose men who would be fair, and who would see that all the widows had whatever they needed.[3]

In Jerusalem a wonderful thing happened. The seven men that everyone chose to take care of the widows all had Greek names! The Aramaic-speaking Christians knew that since everyone understood how they felt, the Greek-speaking Christians would be fair.

[3] *Here's what the early Christians did to solve the problem of people being hurt and angry when they weren't treated fairly. Which of these things do you suppose was most important, and why?*

1. The Greek-speaking Christians told the leaders how they felt.

2. The leaders listened and called everyone together to hear how the Greek people felt.

3. The leaders didn't get angry or blame people for how they felt, or blame the others for what they had done. Instead the leaders tried to solve the problem.

4. The leaders and the people figured out a way to be sure everyone was treated fairly.

Do you think we could use a plan like this in our family, to help solve problems that come when someone feels he or she isn't treated fairly?

Action Idea Discuss the idea of setting up a family council. You can set up family council rules, based on what happened in the Acts church. Possible rules are:

1. Everyone can tell parents how they feel, and ask for a family council.
2. At the council, everyone can tell how they feel about what is happening.
3. No one can blame other people. Instead the council will try to understand why there is a problem.
4. The family council will try to figure out a way for everyone to feel he or she is treated fairly.

In Bible times bread was the most important food of all. It was baked in small loaves, like our rolls. It was also baked flat, like a pancake. You can go to a store with your mom or dad and find that same kind of flat bread sold today. It's called *pita* bread, and it tastes good!

Stephen Is Killed
Acts 6, 7

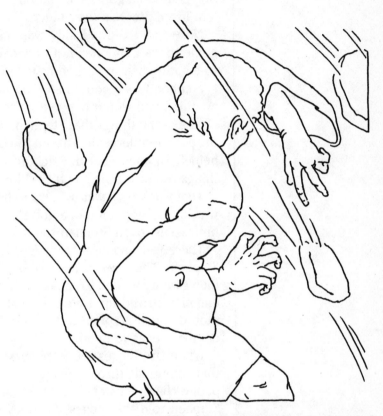

Why do good people like Stephen die?

Background   A death in the family is always difficult for children. It is most difficult if the person who dies is a parent, or a brother or sister. Somehow even children expect older people to die. But sudden, unexpected deaths are disruptive and traumatic.

The story of Stephen, retold especially to be used after the sudden death of a loved one, does not include talkables. It is intended simply to be told, without discussion. Later your child may ask for the story again. Or later he may want to talk about the story. The *Action Idea* suggestion gives several themes from the story that you may pick up and talk about, when your child is ready.

241

"**I**t's Stephen," the old lady said happily.

Stephen was one of the men in the Jerusalem church who helped take care of widows and orphans. Stephen was a good man, and the Christians in Jerusalem loved Stephen very much.

No wonder the old lady was happy to see Stephen come to visit. Stephen not only saw to it she had food to eat; Stephen took time to talk with her, too.

Stephen was a good man. And no one expected that anything bad would happen to Stephen.

One of the things that Stephen liked to do was to tell the people of Jerusalem about the Lord Jesus. God even helped Stephen heal the sick and do other wonderful things to show how much God loved Stephen.

That was why it was so hard to believe when Stephen was killed. Stephen was a good man, and people loved him. Jesus loved Stephen too.

There were some men in Jerusalem who didn't like Stephen. These were men who had hated Jesus and didn't want Stephen to speak about the Lord. Finally the enemies stirred up a mob against Stephen. The angry mob dragged Stephen to the very court that had condemned Jesus to death.

When the judges let Stephen speak, he boldly told them how, all through history, God's Old Testament people hadn't listened to God or obeyed the Lord. Stephen told the judges that they had done the most terrible thing of all. God had sent His Son, Jesus. Instead of loving God's Son, those judges betrayed and murdered Jesus.

Everything Stephen said was true. Because it was true, the judges on the court were furious. They howled in anger and glared at Stephen.

Then Stephen looked toward the heavens and saw Jesus! "Look," Stephen said. "I see heaven open, and the Son of Man, Jesus, standing at the right hand of God the Father."

The judges of the court and Stephen's other enemies

were so angry! They yelled at the top of their voices and dragged Stephen outside the city.

Stephen was a good man. Stephen was a man whom all the Christians in Jerusalem loved. Stephen was a man whom God loved. Stephen hadn't lied, or done anything wrong. Stephen had only told the judges of the court the truth.

Even though Stephen was a good man, the crowd dragged Stephen outside the city and began to throw great rocks at him. The stones knocked Stephen to his knees. Stephen knew that he was going to be killed.

Then Stephen looked up to heaven and asked Jesus to forgive the people who killed him. And Stephen died.

How sorrowful the Christians in Jerusalem must have been. Stephen was just a young man; he wasn't old enough to die. Stephen was a good man, whom everyone loved. God hadn't been punishing Stephen. God loved Stephen too.

No one in Jerusalem knew just why Stephen had to die so young. But everyone was glad for one thing. Stephen was with Jesus in heaven. Stephen was gone, and everyone would miss Stephen very much. But Stephen was with Jesus. Someday the Christians of Jerusalem would see Stephen again.

Action Idea When telling this story the first time, it's probably best to make no comments unless your child raises questions. It's probable that, if the story meets a need, your boy or girl will ask for the story again. After the second or third retelling, you may want to talk, as comfortingly as possible, about the person who has died in your family.

Talk quickly about ways that person was like Stephen. He or she was a good person. He or she was loved by the family. He or she was loved by God too. We don't know why he or she died. But we do know that God loved him or her, and that he or she is now with Jesus.

Paul and Barnabas Break Up
Acts 15:36–41

Can arguments hurt so much that people have to break up?

Background Divorce by mom and dad can be a shattering experience for children. Research has shown that divorce is always harmful, though not necessarily as harmful as staying together may be. Our challenge when a divorce does take place is to minimize any damage to the children.

There is no Bible story that deals directly with divorce. But the report of the argument which led to the breaking up of the missionary team of Paul and Barnabas contains many parallels.

There is little indication here that one was "right" while the other was "wrong." Both were probably to blame for the painful separation that took place. It is doubly significant that each of the men was a godly leader, and each continued in leadership in the early church. It's tempting for us to think that if they had only followed principles of reconciliation that each taught, some compromise could have been worked out.

But it didn't happen that way.

As in so many families these days, a time came when the two, who had bonded their lives together, came to that painful point at which they felt they must separate.

Without condoning or condemning, this story is to help your children discover the parallels between Paul and Barnabas' breakup and your divorce. It is to help your children begin that essential process of talking about their thoughts and feelings, which will help them cope with the reality of what has happened in your family.

244

"You can't be together as long as Paul and Barnabas have, and then just break up."

At least, that's what people at the church in Antioch thought when Paul and Barnabas began to have terrible arguments.

Why, Paul and Barnabas had been together for years, traveling as Christian missionaries. Paul and Barnabas had worked together, and eaten together, and preached together, and prayed together for years. People who have been together for years just don't break up. At least, that's what the people at Antioch thought. Besides, Paul and Barnabas did love each other. They had been the best of friends. When you've been so close, how can you ever break up?[1]

What happened with Paul and Barnabas was that they had a disagreement. Barnabas and Paul were planning to go back as missionaries, to visit churches they had started before. Barnabas wanted to take along a helper named Mark. But Mark had gone with Paul and Barnabas once before, and Mark had quit when he was needed. Paul didn't think he could trust Mark to be a good helper.

It may not seem like much to argue about. But it was very important to Barnabas that Mark be given a second chance. And it was very important to Paul that any helper be trustworthy.[2]

We don't know how good the reasons Paul and Barnabas had for breaking up were. We do know that neither one was happy about arguing. When people care about each other and have been together a long time, it's very hard to decide to break up. But finally the arguments became so bad, and Paul and Barnabas hurt each other so much, that they parted company.

Barnabas took Mark and went to Cyprus to be a missionary. Paul took a helper named Silas, and Paul went to a different country to be a missionary.

Both Paul and Barnabas felt badly about their argument. They felt badly about breaking up. But Paul and

[1] *Do you suppose people who have been as close as Paul and Barnabas—very, very good friends—can break up? What do you think makes people who care for each other break up?*

[2] *What are some of the things you think people might break up over? What do you think are the most important reasons people have for breaking up?*

[3] Breaking up always hurts people in some ways. Divorce is breaking up, and often people feel hurt. (Talk about some of the ways you feel hurt, and your ex-spouse felt hurt.) What are some of the ways that breaking up made you feel hurt?

Barnabas must have felt that breaking up was the best thing to do.[3]

While it always hurts when people break up after being together for a long time, we have to believe when it happens that it will be for the best. God was with Paul and Silas, and God was with Barnabas and Mark too. Barnabas did help Mark become a trustworthy and faithful Christian. In fact, that Mark is the same Mark who wrote the Gospel of Mark that we have in our Bible. So God was with each person after they broke up. God loved Paul and Barnabas after they broke up, just as God loved them while they were together.

> *Action Idea* This story will indicate your readiness to talk about feelings children may have about the divorce. Even though it is likely to be painful for you, do encourage children to share their feelings. Your boys and girls can cope with divorce. A new base of security is most likely to be developed when you communicate freely about this painful experience, which has affected you all.

Paul Stays Sick
2 Corinthians 12:7–10

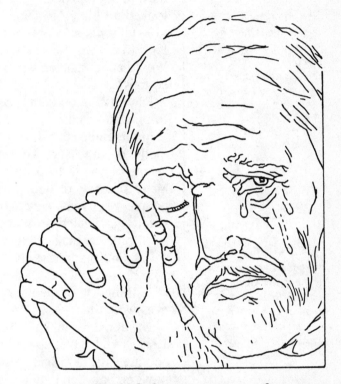

Would God say no to a prayer from someone Jesus loves?

Background Unanswered prayers usually trouble parents more than they do children. Very seldom is the faith of our boys and girls disturbed when God says "No" to one of their requests. But there are times, when a great need exists, and a prayer isn't answered the way we yearn, that disappointment may stimulate doubt or even anger.

This *talkable Bible story* relates a "No" answer to prayer given the apostle Paul. Paul had healed so many sick persons. But Paul himself was not healed from a debilitating disease which many biblical scholars believe was an eye disease. Paul's experience, and Paul's response to it, can help our children realize that "No" is a possible answer to the most heartfelt prayer. Even "No" can be an expression of love. God will never abandon us in our hurts.

247

Paul's eyes hurt.

Paul wanted to rub his eyes so badly. But the apostle Paul didn't rub his eyes. He knew it would only make them hurt worse.

Paul peered out of his swollen, watering eyes, trying hard to see the people he was talking with. The people looked all blurry to Paul. What was worse, Paul knew how ugly his swollen, red and watery eyes made him look to others. He wanted to tell people about Jesus. Would anyone listen when his sickness made Paul look so ugly?

Paul just hated being so sick. He wanted desperately to be well again.[1]

In this Bible story Paul is the apostle Paul, who wrote many of our New Testament letters. It must have seemed strange to people that this Paul was so sick. Many times Paul had prayed, and God healed other people who were sick. You would have thought that Paul, who healed so many other people, would have been able to make himself well without any trouble.

But Paul hadn't really healed anyone. It was Jesus who healed when Paul prayed. So now Paul did a very wise thing. He prayed and asked the Lord to make his eyes well.[2]

The apostle Paul knew that God loved him. Paul loved Jesus, too. He had spent his whole life teaching others about Jesus. God had answered many, many of Paul's prayers. So when Paul prayed that God would make his eyes well, he really expected God to do it. And soon.

But Paul didn't begin to get well.

Paul prayed, but his eyes remained red and swollen. Paul prayed, but he still looked ugly. Paul still had trouble seeing the people he talked with about Jesus.

So Paul prayed again, and again. He pleaded with the Lord to make him well. He wanted so very, very badly to get well again. But still Paul didn't begin to get well.[3]

The apostle Paul wanted to be healed so very badly. But God said "No" to Paul's prayer.

Then God told the apostle something very special.

[1] What are some of the feelings Paul must have had when he was sick? Are they like the feelings you have because you (or dad, mom and so on) are sick?

[2] What do you suppose will happen when Paul prays? How many reasons can you think of why the Lord would answer Paul's prayer, and make Paul well again?

[3] How do you suppose Paul felt, after praying so hard, and not beginning to get well? (Together list a number of feelings.) What feelings have you had when God hasn't answered some of your prayers? It's very hard when God says "No" to something we want very badly.

And Paul wrote it down in the Bible, for you and me. God told Paul the Lord would give Paul enough grace to be able to live with his sickness. God promised that when Paul felt the weakest, God would be there to give him strength.

Paul's being sick didn't mean that God did not love Paul. Not at all. Bad things that happen to us don't mean that God has stopped loving us, either.

In fact, God can be even more real to us when we are weak. Then we know how much we need God's help.

But it helped Paul to know that God still loved him, even though he didn't get better. After a time Paul even began to feel glad about his sickness. "When I am weak," Paul wrote in the Bible, "then I am strong." Paul knew that God helped Paul be strong and cheerful and loving in spite of the sickness. And Paul knew God loved him. Even when Paul was sick.

> ***Action Idea*** If you tell this Bible story during a serious family illness after you and the children have prayed together often for healing, you'll not need any particular follow-up process. The Scripture will have its own ministry and help your boys and girls realize that God hasn't abandoned them. None of you may understand the "why" of the sickness. But the Bible's affirmation of God's love, and of His commitment to strengthen you in your trial, will be healing and reassuring.

What Is Heaven Like?
Various Bible Passages

What is the most beautiful scene you can imagine?

Background Heaven remains a dominant image in Christian faith. The promise of eternal life is ours, and even our children have questions about what eternity will bring. This story is designed to deal with children's curiosity about the future life after the traumatic emotions have subsided and new, normal patterns of life have been reestablished.

Everybody has some idea of what heaven is like. But it's hard for us to know for sure just what it will be like when we are there. We do know that we'll be with our friends and family who love Jesus. And we do know that God will be there with us. Most people have some other ideas too about what heaven will be like.[1]

Let me read you some of the words in the Bible that tell us about heaven. In the Old Testament Book of Isaiah (65:17–25) God tells us about a wonderful new world He will make. Here is what God tells us:

> Behold, I will create
>   new heavens and a new earth.
> The former things will not be
>   remembered,
>   nor will they come to mind.
> But be glad and rejoice forever
>   in what I will create. . .
> the sound of weeping and of crying
>   will be heard in it no more.
> Never again will there be in it
>   an infant who lives but a few days,
>   or an old man who does not live out
>   his years. . . .
> They will build houses and dwell in them:
>   they will plant vineyards and eat their fruit. . . .
> They will not toil in vain
>   or bear children doomed to misfortune;
> for they will be a people blessed by the
>   Lord. . . .
> The wolf and the lamb will feed together,
>   and the lion will eat straw like the ox. . . .
> They will neither harm nor destroy
>   on all my holy mountain.

The New Testament Book of Revelation talks about heaven too. Here are some of the things the Bible says about heaven in Revelation 21 and 22:

[1] *What do you suppose heaven is like? (Distribute paper and crayons to all family members, including yourself.) Let's draw a picture of what we think heaven may be like, and how we'll feel there. (When the pictures are completed, have each person tell about what he or she has drawn, and explain his or her picture.)*

I saw a new heaven and a new earth, for the first heaven and earth had passed away, and there was no longer any sea. I saw the Holy City, the new Jerusalem, coming down out of heaven from God. . . . I heard a loud voice from [God's] throne saying, Now the dwelling of God is with men, and he will live with them. They will be his people, and God himself will be with them and be their God. God will wipe away every tear from their eyes. There will be no more death or mourning or crying or pain, for the old order of things has passed away. . . .

The city does not need the sun or moon to shine on it, for the glory of God gives it light, . . . On no day will its gates ever be shut, for there will be no night there. . . . Nothing impure will ever enter it, nor will anyone who does what is shameful or deceitful. . . . Then the angel showed me the river of the water of life, as clear as crystal, flowing from the throne of God and of the Lamb, down the middle of the great street of the city. On each side of the river stood the tree of life, bearing twelve crops of fruit, yielding its fruit every month. And the leaves of the tree are for the healing of the nations. No longer will there be any curse. The throne of God and the Lamb will be in the city, and his servants will serve him. They will see his face, and his name will be on their foreheads. There will be no more night. They will not need the light of a lamp or the light of the sun, for the Lord God will give them light. And they will rule for ever and ever (21:1–4, 23, 25, 27; 22:1–4).[2]

[2] What are some of the things you learned about heaven? How is what the Bible says like the picture you drew? How is what the Bible said not like your picture? If we were to make a family mural—a very big picture that we all drew and painted together—what would we want to show on that picture-mural?

Let's read through the Bible passages again. Whenever you hear something you think ought to go on a picture-mural, stop me and we'll write it down.

(Reread the passages, letting your children take notes).[3]

Let's thank God that He love us so much that He's prepared a wonderful place for us to be, forever and forever.

[3] Which of the things about heaven do you suppose you'll like best?

Action Idea Make a "heaven" mural together. Let each family member represent things about heaven that seem special to him or her on a single mural

Index

254

sheet. Use crayons or water-based paints to create your mural.

We will not be able to accurately represent the wonderful eternity God has planned for us. But a sense of assurance and comfort will be ours as we focus on the endless love of God for Jesus' people.

Being fair with others, Acts 6, *238*
Breaking up with friends, Acts 15, *244*

Giving
The use of allowances, Mark 12, *197*
Giving to meet others' needs, Acts 4, *235*
Guilt
Feeling bad when we do wrong, Gen. 3, *26*
Consequences of doing wrong, Num. 13, 14, *62*

Jealousy
Of brothers or sisters, Gen. 37, *50*
Understanding its impact, 1 Sam. 18, *96*
Accepting individual differences, Luke 10, *175*
Deciding on what is fair, Acts 6, *238*

Listening
Listening to each other, Gen. 18, *41*; Acts 6, *238*
Developing listening skills, 1 Sam. 3, *80*; Acts 15, *244*
Jesus listens when we pray, Luke 18, *194*
Lies
Surrendering to peer pressure, Matt. 26, *209*

Moving
Reducing fears about moving, Gen. 12, *29*
Defining "home" as family; people rather than a place, Ruth, *77*
Moral development
Choosing what is right, Gen. 3, *23*; Gen. 39–41, *53*; 1 Sam. 24, 26, *102*; Esther, *123*; Acts 4, *232*
Consequences of wrong, Gen. 3, *26*
Acting from faith, not fear, Gen. 12, 20, *32*
Limits on expression of anger, Gen. 37, *50*
Doing right despite peer pressure, Josh. 5, 6, *71*
Doing right despite fears, Judges 6, *74*; 1 Sam. 13, 15, *86*
Dealing with anger, 1 Sam. 25, *99*
Valuing people more than things, 1 Kings 21, *114*; Luke 12, *182*; Luke 12, *185*

The role of discipline, Jonah, *134*
Acting in view of Jesus' presence, John 1, *154*
Developing sensitivity to others, Mark 1, *160*; Luke 10, *172*
Developing responsibility, Matt. 25, *200*
Learning to express love, Acts 2, *229*; Acts 4, *235*

Peer pressure
Doing right despite peer pressure, Josh. 5, 6, *71*; 1 Sam. 24, 26, *102*; Matt. 26, *209*
Fear of what others might think, 1 Sam. 13, 15, *86*
Good friends can help us do right, Daniel 1, *127*
Prayer
Telling God all our feelings, Gen. 18, *41*
Praying for healing, 2 Kings 20, *120*; John 4, *157*
Unanswered prayers for healing, 2 Cor. 12, *247*
Praying when we have done wrong, Jonah, *134*
Understanding the Lord's prayer, Luke 11, *179*
Jesus listens when we pray, Luke 18, *194*
God answers with what is best, Matt. 26, *203*
Praying for help, Acts 4, *232*
Promises
Finding God's promises to us, Gen. 15, *38*
God's promise to send Jesus, Isaiah 7, *137*
Punishment
As a consequence of wrongdoing, Num. 13, 14, *62*
Intended to help us do right, Jonah, *134*

Quarreling
Dealing with sibling disputes, Gen. 13, *35*

Rejection
Helping children deal with rejection, Luke 4, *166*
Responsibility, for own actions
No "good excuses", Gen. 3, *26*
Responsibility, as a trait
Use of chores to develop, Matt. 25, *200*

Index